The Art of Non-Sexual Foreplay

book 1 - a guide for men

Nolan Collins

Nolan Collins

Contents

DISCLAIMER

The information contained within this book or my website is not a substitute for professional advice such as from a medical doctor, psychiatrist, therapist or counsellor. The information provided does not constitute legal or professional advice, nor is it intended to be.

Diagnosing psychological or medical conditions is for trained medical professionals (physicians and therapists).

Any decisions you make and the consequences thereof are your own. Under no circumstances can you hold Nolan Collins or RAMPIT Solutions Ltd liable for your actions.

This book is dedicated to the women of the world waiting for a good man. We are here, and I hope this book creates a few more. You deserve it.

Introduction

The Intimacy Manual No One Gave You

Let's address the elephant in the bedroom: None of us received a manual on creating intimacy. When most people hear the word "foreplay," their minds jump to dim lights and moments just before sex. But real foreplay—the kind that builds deep intimacy and keeps passion alive—is so much more.

Think about it. We spend years learning calculus, memorising the elements of the periodic table, and knowing that mitochondria are the powerhouse of the cell, but somehow "How to Make Your Partner Feel Desired Without Taking Off Their Clothes - For Beginners!" never made it onto the curriculum.

Instead, our intimacy "education" consisted of rom-coms where couples magically transition from fighting to ripping each other's clothes off, or awkward talks where parents mumbled something about "when two people love each other very much." Congratulations! You've probably inherited these patterns like an unwanted subscription to "Bad Touch Monthly."

Introduction

By adulthood, most of us are operating with:

- Intimacy ideas we absorbed from media that skips straight to bedroom gymnastics
- Foreplay techniques that consist mainly of "maybe if I stare at them intensely enough, they'll know what I want"
- A deep-seated belief that physical affection must always lead to sex
- The relationship equivalent of a chef who only knows how to make one dish—and it's always undercooked

Sensuality is one of the great, lost arts of modern relationships. Somewhere along the way, it became confused with sexuality, as if the only point of touch or tenderness is to rush toward intimacy. But sensuality is something else entirely—it's the quiet everlasting language of connection. It's about listening to her, not just with your ears, but with your presence, your actions, and yes, your touch.

Here's the thing: women crave touch, but only the right kind of touch. And for those who say they don't like touch, chances are they've experienced the wrong kind. No woman wants to feel like she's being approached by Dr. Octavius, all frantic hands and zero finesse. This is not the time to swoop in with eight overactive limbs and start pawing at her like a dog digging for a bone instead of a partner. Sensuality isn't about doing more—it's about doing less and doing it thoughtfully. A well-placed touch says, I see you, and I want you to feel cherished.

Welcome to **The Art of Nonsexual Foreplay**, where we flip the script on what intimacy means. It's the sum of a hundred little actions that make her feel seen, respected, and adored. It's the touch of your hand on her back as you guide her into a room, the way you remember her favourite snack, and the lingering eye contact during a quiet moment. These gestures aren't about seduction; they're about connection.

Non-sexual foreplay has become a lost art, replaced by a culture of impatience and ego-driven expectations. **Too many men act like boys,** rushing in with clumsy hands, hoping for a reward without first understanding what their partner truly needs. But here's the truth: a man knows when to pause, when to look, when to linger. He knows when she needs a small moment of attention to feel seen and loved, not because he expects something in return, but because she matters.

This isn't just a book of tips and tricks; it's a guide to creating a relationship where your partner feels valued, safe, and understood. It's about mastering the subtle art of making someone feel seen in ways that deepen emotional and physical bonds without crossing into overtly sexual territory.

Women don't want a partner who's only there for the easy parts or the big moments. They want a man who's present for the little things: the well-timed arm around her, the squeeze of her hand when she needs reassurance, the way he notices her without her having to ask. They want a man who adds to her life, not one who expects rewards for simply showing up.

Here's the truth: intimacy doesn't start in the bedroom. It starts when she feels like she's the most important person in your world. It's built in the micro-moments when you notice her, show up for her, and communicate that you care. These gestures create the foundation for trust, safety, and connection —the real aphrodisiacs of any relationship.

The right kind of man puts his ego aside. He doesn't touch her to keep score or act like he's completing a checklist. His gestures are clear, confident, and focused on her—not as a means to an end, but as an expression of love, respect, and attention. Women notice this. They feel it when a man is intentional in his actions, when his presence is strong and reassuring.

While the immediate goal of these actions isn't physical intimacy, it's the accumulation of these seemingly small habits that transforms your relationship over time. When physical intimacy does happen, it becomes infinitely more powerful because you've already established a language of connection. The ground between you is fertile with meaning, trust, and mutual understanding.

And the irony: the more you focus on making her feel safe, valued, and beautiful, the more she'll naturally reciprocate. When you act like a gentleman, she'll respond in kind, and the touch, affection, and support you crave will come back to you without you even having to ask. It's not manipulation— it's connection. The better you make her feel about herself, the more she'll reflect that positivity back to you. Who would have guessed?

Think of these gestures as compound interest for your relationship. Each small deposit might seem insignificant in the moment, but over time, they build a wealth of intimacy that pays dividends in every aspect of your connection. When moments of physical intimacy do arise, they're not isolated events but extensions of the connection you've been cultivating all along—richer, easier, and more profound because you've been practicing intimacy in a hundred different ways.

Sensuality isn't about you—it's about her. It's not about what your friends have told you to do, or what social media says women want. It's about listening, paying attention, and learning her language of love. Maybe it's a hand lightly brushing her cheek as she speaks. Maybe it's pulling her close without words to remind her she's safe. Or maybe it's just sitting beside her in silence and letting your knees touch. The magic is in knowing that every small gesture counts when it's done with intention.

It's like trying to create a gourmet meal after only watching competitive eating contests. Sure, you've seen someone devour a plate of food, but that doesn't qualify you to create a five-course dining experience. The result? Two people desperately wanting connection but having no idea how to create the delicious simmer of anticipation and appreciation that makes intimacy—both in and out of the bedroom—so much more satisfying.

And here's where it gets even better: once you've mastered these moments, you can take them deeper. Imagine the effect of these gestures when she's just stepped out of the shower, her skin warm and soft. Imagine touching her gently in the morning, making her feel like your first thought. Or pausing in bed, tracing your fingertips along her shoulder, just to let her know how much she means to you. This isn't about rushing—it's about savoring the connection and letting her know she's your world.

This book isn't just for men looking to romance their partners; it's for anyone who wants to understand how to nurture a relationship that feels alive, playful, and deeply meaningful. Whether you're in a new relationship or you've been married for years, the 104 gestures and accompanying insights in this book will help you turn ordinary moments into extraordinary connections.

So, take a breath. Slow down. Approach her not with haste, but with the confidence of someone who knows that love, intimacy, and connection are built in the quiet moments. These gestures aren't about impressing her—they're about making her feel safe, adored, and truly seen. When you listen to her needs and act with clarity and intention, you'll create a bond that deepens over time. Because in the end, the better you treat her, the better your relationship will feel for both of you.

Because it's never too late to learn that the most erogenous zone is actually the space between casual touch and sexual expectation—that delicious territory where intimacy thrives without demanding anything more. And it's never too early to start building the habits that make those moments of physical connection not just possible, but transcendent.

Before we dive into the specifics, let's talk about **how to make these actions work**. Because while a thoughtful gesture can be powerful, how you deliver it is just as important as the gesture itself.

If your partner has given you this book as a gift, it's because they know how much you love them and already do for them, yet may be doing the same few things. Like any skill, learning new tools and perspectives can increase your efficiency, so take this gift as a compliment, to complement what you're already doing and add some variety to your toolbox of love.

And a note for the ladies: If you find this book and realise all those things he's been doing are coming from here, there is only one thing I can suggest: Smile to yourself and know that he loves you and cares about you enough to WANT to do more. If there's something you like that he hasn't done, suggest it in passing (not in anger with "you NEVER do..."). Then put the book back where you found it and enjoy the attention he offers.

If you want to know what you can do for him, and trust me it's not the same as what he can do for you, then check out book 2 of the Art of Nonsexual Foreplay - a guide for women - see the resources at the back of the book.

Introduction

Welcome to the art of non-sexual foreplay. Your relationship is about to get a lot more interesting, one gentle touch at a time.

One more thing...

This book is written under the assumption you actually like each other and want to do more for her. Trying some of this if she's reading books on how to get away with murder under the guise of writing a bestselling novel probably won't help. If this is the case I suggest looking at the resources at the back of the book first and coming back to this one!

11 Tips to Make These Gestures Work Better

Gentlemen, before you dive into the 100 gestures that follow, let's talk about execution. Just as a chef needs to understand technique before creating a masterpiece, you need to grasp these fundamentals before your actions can truly resonate. Here's how to transform simple moments into powerful connection points:

1. Master the Art of the Pause

Great connections aren't rushed. When you're about to brush her hair from her face or touch her hand, pause for a beat. That moment of stillness heightens the significance of the gesture, giving her time to notice and feel its weight. A pause says, "I'm fully here with you." It also lets you gauge her response—whether she leans into the moment or pulls back slightly, you'll know exactly where you stand.

Why it works: Anticipation amplifies the emotional impact of the action, making even small moments feel monumental. Women often experience the world more through anticipation than men do—use this to your advantage.

2. Perfect the Power of Eye Contact

Eye contact isn't just looking at someone—it's seeing them. Hold her gaze for an extra second when you compliment her or during a quiet moment. This unspoken connection says everything words can't. But remember, no creepy staring contests. This is intimacy, not an interrogation. If you're unsure, start small—catch her eye across the room and pair it with a warm smile that reaches your eyes.

Why it works: Eyes are a gateway to trust and vulnerability. They speak volumes without a single word. Many men miss this opportunity, looking away too quickly or avoiding eye contact altogether.

3. Touch with Intention

Not all touch is created equal. The difference between a fleeting pat and a lingering hand on her shoulder is night and day. Think of touch like a spectrum: light brushes for playfulness, firm contact for reassurance, and everything in between for moments of connection. Even something as simple as tracing patterns on her palm can spark a feeling of closeness when done with care and presence.

Why it works: Thoughtful, intentional touch communicates care and attentiveness, signaling that you're fully present. Women can immediately sense the difference between absent-minded touching and deliberate connection.

4. Notice the Little Things

Did she change her hair? Wear a new perfume? Mention something she's excited about? Noticing and bringing up these small details tells her, "I see you." It's not about flattery; it's about showing you're tuned in to her world. Something as simple as saying, "That colour looks amazing on you," can make her feel appreciated in a way that resonates all day. The more specific your observation, the more powerful its impact.

2

Why it works: Feeling seen is one of the most powerful ways to build trust and connection. In a world where people often feel invisible, your attention is a rare gift.

5. Let Silence Speak

Some of the most intimate moments don't need words. Resting your forehead against hers, holding her hand, or simply sitting close says more than a thousand compliments ever could. Silence lets emotions breathe. It can also create a space for her to share what's on her mind without feeling rushed. Many men feel compelled to fill silence—resist this urge and discover the power of shared quiet.

Why it works: Stillness invites closeness and allows her to feel safe in your presence. It demonstrates security and confidence that many men miss in their rush to speak or act.

6. Add Playfulness to the Mix

Romance isn't always serious. A silly dance, a playful tease, or a shared laugh can bring lightness and warmth to your connection. Don't take yourself too seriously—fun is a cornerstone of intimacy. A quick moment of levity can ease tension and remind her that being with you is as enjoyable as it is meaningful. Be willing to look foolish occasionally—it shows confidence and authenticity.

Why it works: Laughter creates bonds, releases tension, and keeps things fresh and exciting. Women are often attracted to men who can make them laugh, not because they're comedians, but because humour signals intelligence and emotional awareness.

7. Use Your Voice Wisely

Whispering something sweet or funny just for her creates an intimate bubble no one else can enter. Your voice—its tone, volume, and words—can set the mood and make her feel like she's the center of your attention. Even a quiet "I've been thinking about you all day" can make an ordinary moment extraordinary. Lower your voice slightly when speaking intimately—it creates an immediate sense of closeness.

Why it works: The sound of your voice, especially when it's soft and intentional, is inherently soothing and personal. Many men don't realise the powerful effect their voice can have when used with awareness.

8. Understand the Timing

Even the sweetest gesture can flop if it's poorly timed. If she's stressed or distracted, save the moment for when she can fully appreciate it. Thoughtfulness isn't just about what you do—it's about when you do it. For example, slipping a kind note into her bag before a busy day can mean more than trying to cheer her up mid-chaos. Learn to read her emotional state and respond accordingly.

Why it works: Timing ensures your actions land with the impact they deserve. Women often report that what makes a gesture special isn't just the action itself, but how perfectly timed it was to their needs.

9. Be Consistent, Not Overwhelming

A single grand gesture is lovely, but consistent small actions are what truly build intimacy. Don't try to do all 100 gestures in one week—it's not a marathon. Pace yourself, and let these moments happen naturally. A pattern of thoughtfulness shows her you're present in her life for the long haul, not just the highlights. Remember: sustainability trumps intensity every time.

Why it works: Steady care fosters trust and keeps the relationship grounded. Too many men oscillate between complete inattention and overwhelming focus—find the middle ground of reliable presence.

10. Be Genuine

This one's simple: if you don't mean it, don't do it. Authenticity is the foundation of everything in this book. These gestures should reflect how you truly feel, not what you think you should do. Even a simple, heartfelt, "You're incredible," means more when it's genuine. Women have finely-tuned radars for insincerity—they'll sense it immediately if you're just going through the motions.

Here's a bonus gesture: Show enthusiasm or passion when she gets home! Getting up, opening the door, taking her coat, making her a hot drink, giving a kiss and a hug are all things you can do when she gets home, whether it's from work, an outing or just popping to the corner shop - she'll love it (after she asks if you've been taken over by an alien!)

Why it works: Genuine actions resonate on a deeper level, making her feel truly valued. In a world full of performance and pretense, authenticity is the rarest and most precious gift you can offer.

11. Be creative.

The gestures and support sections are a guide for you to tweak and play with. Think about all the things you like about your partner. What attracted you to her? What makes her stand out? When you see the suggested phrases, don't use them if it feels awkward. Instead, think of something you would say that will resonate more than a scripted phrase.

Why it works: Only you know your mind, and your partner. Getting creative opens up each gesture to more angles and ways to deliver them that work specifically for you.

Remember, gentlemen: these aren't tricks or manipulations—they're skills. Like any worthwhile ability, they take practice and intention. The difference between a man who merely attempts these gestures and one who masters them is attention to these fundamentals. Your relationship deserves that level of care.

"But Nolan, I already do a few of these, isn't that enough?" - Would you want the same three meals every week? or only watch the same four TV shows? It gets predictable and boring. Thats why this book isn't "ten things you can do to impress your partner"! 100 gives you variety, opportunities for spontaneity (in her eyes) and helps you build a repertoire of sensuality even your grandfather coudn't teach you. Yes, they were better at this than we are today!

Quick note: Some of these may seem similar, yet are distinctly different, either in intention, touch, pace or situation.

Now, armed with these principles, let's explore the 100 gestures that will transform your relationship one thoughtful moment at a time.

Chapter 1
Placing a Hand on the Small of Her Back

Why It Helps

There are few women who don't lean—figuratively or literally —into a well-timed hand on the small of their back. It's an understated yet incredibly grounding gesture that says, *I see you. I'm here for you.* Done right, it's not possessive but protective, offering a quiet sense of security as you guide her through a doorway or across a busy space. It's the kind of touch that feels natural but lingers in her mind long after.

This isn't about theatrics or overthinking; it's about being quietly present. The small of the back is also uniquely intimate without being sexual—a place rarely touched by others, making your connection there feel distinctly meaningful. It's one of those gestures that feels almost cinematic—a little move that belongs in every love story, including yours.

Phrase to Say

"I love the feeling of walking beside you." OR "You're the most important thing in this room."

Tips to Make It Work

- **Eye Contact:** Glance at her when you do this, even briefly. That tiny connection says, *I'm thinking of you, not just guiding you.*
- **Touch:** Keep it gentle and deliberate, like a whisper, not a shout. Your palm should rest lightly—you're not steering her; you're supporting her.
- **Humour:** If the moment allows, add a playful comment like, "I should start charging for bodyguard services."

When to Use

This gesture works beautifully when entering a restaurant, navigating a crowded space, or guiding her through a doorway. It's equally effective in casual settings or formal events, though the pressure of your touch might vary—lighter for formal occasions, slightly more present for casual moments.

Chapter 2
Brushing a Strand of Hair from Her Face

Why It Helps

There's something undeniably intimate about this small act. For a moment, the world shrinks to just the two of you. Brushing a strand of hair from her face says, *I notice the little things about you, and I care*. It's delicate, thoughtful, and quietly romantic. Few gestures are as simple yet as powerful, leaving her feeling cherished without a single word spoken.

The key is to approach this with softness, like you're handling something fragile. Timing matters too—do this when the moment feels naturally tender, not rushed or forced. Done right, it's a move that feels as much about who she is as how she looks.

Phrase to Say

"This deserves to be seen." OR "Even the wind can't help but reach for you."

Tips to Make It Work

- **Eye Contact:** Lock eyes as your hand lingers briefly. It's that pause that creates the magic.
- **Touch:** Be gentle—your fingers should barely graze her skin, like a whisper of connection.
- **Humour:** If the moment allows, tease her with, "You're a walking shampoo commercial, you know that?"

When to Use

This gesture shines in quiet, intimate moments—perhaps when you're sitting close in conversation, sharing a private laugh, or during a natural pause in your day. It works especially well when you've caught her in a candid moment, slightly disheveled but wholly beautiful.

Chapter 3
Opening a Door and Holding It for Her

Why It Helps

It might seem old-fashioned, but opening a door for her is a timeless gesture of respect and care. It's not about suggesting she can't open it herself—it's about showing that you want to make even the smallest moments in her day a little easier. This seemingly ordinary act communicates extraordinary attentiveness when done with intention rather than obligation.

The beauty of this gesture lies in its simplicity and the message beneath: *I'm thinking about you before myself.* In a world where self-absorption is common, this momentary prioritisation of her comfort stands out. It demonstrates both respect and protection—two qualities women consistently find attractive in men.

Phrase to Say

"For the most important person in my day." OR "This door's not good enough for you, but it'll do."

Tips to Make It Work

- **Eye Contact:** As she walks through, meet her gaze for a second. That simple acknowledgment transforms a routine courtesy into a personal connection.
- **Touch:** If the moment feels right, let your hand lightly graze the small of her back as she passes—bridging the gesture from polite to intimate.
- **humour:** For a playful twist, you might say, "If I had my way, rose petals would fall every time you walked through a doorway."

When to Use

This gesture works in virtually any setting—from casual coffee shops to elegant restaurants. It's particularly powerful when unexpected: opening her car door, holding the elevator door, or even opening a door at home when her hands are full. The key is consistency; make it a habit rather than a special occasion gesture.

Chapter 4
Sharing a Quiet, Knowing Smile Across the Room

Why It Helps

In a crowded room, a private smile creates invisible threads of connection that only you two can feel. This gesture tells her that despite physical distance and the presence of others, your awareness is centered on her. It creates a secret world between you—a world where only you two hold the key.

What makes this particularly powerful is the element of witness without possession. You're seeing her in her element, perhaps laughing with friends or engaged in conversation, and your smile acknowledges both her independence and your connection to her. The hint of mystery in a smile from across the room often creates more intrigue than an hour of conversation.

Phrase to Say

This gesture works without words, but if you're texting her later: "Seeing you smile across the room tonight was my favourite moment." OR "You have no idea what that smile of yours does to me."

Tips to Make It Work

- **Eye Contact:** Don't stare continuously—catch her eye naturally, hold for a meaningful second or two, then return to your conversation. The intermittent quality creates anticipation.
- **Body Language:** Slightly tilt your head or raise an eyebrow to add a layer of meaning to your smile— curiosity, admiration, or playfulness.
- **Timing:** Choose a moment when she's comfortable but not deeply engaged in conversation—you want to enhance her experience, not distract from it.

When to Use

This gesture is perfect for social gatherings, parties, or any setting where you're separated by space but connected by awareness. It works during family gatherings, work events, or when one of you is busy with a task while the other observes appreciatively.

Chapter 5
Bringing Her a Warm Drink Unexpectedly

Why It Helps

There's something deeply nurturing about being handed a perfectly prepared warm drink. It's a small gesture that speaks volumes: *I was thinking about you. I know what brings you comfort. I went out of my way to bring it to you.* The warmth of the cup mirrors the warmth of the sentiment behind it.

What elevates this beyond simple courtesy is the element of surprise and the attention to detail. Remembering exactly how she takes her coffee or which tea she prefers when she's stressed shows that you're paying attention to the small things that make her unique. It's intimacy through observation.

Phrase to Say

"I thought you might need this right about now." OR "Just the way you like it—I was paying attention."

Tips to Make It Work

- **Timing:** The unexpected nature is what makes this special. Bring it when she's working, reading, or just waking up—moments when she might not expect your attention.
- **Details:** Get the specifics right—the exact amount of cream, the precise temperature, her favourite mug. These details transform a nice gesture into a deeply personal one.
- **Delivery:** Hand it to her with both hands, almost ceremonially. This small flourish elevates the moment from functional to meaningful.

When to Use

This gesture works beautifully first thing in the morning, during a stressful workday, or as she's unwinding in the evening. It's particularly powerful during transitional moments in her day—when she's shifting from one mode to another and could use both the comfort and the acknowledgment.

PS. I like to put the kettle on for my partner when I know she's on the way home, and get the cup and her favourite tea ready so I can flip on the kettle for 30 seconds when she pulls up and have the tea ready when she walks in!

Chapter 6
Wrapping Her in a Blanket When She's Cold

Why It Helps

There's something profoundly protective about wrapping someone in warmth. When you notice her slight shiver or see her pull her knees closer to her body and respond by gently placing a blanket around her shoulders, you're saying without words: *I notice your discomfort. Your comfort matters to me. I'm here to take care of you.*

This gesture taps into something primal—the human need for protection from the elements. By addressing this basic need attentively, you create a cascade of emotional warmth that complements the physical warmth of the blanket. It's care in its most tangible form.

Phrase to Say

"Let me warm you up a bit." OR "I noticed you were cold—this should help."

Tips to Make It Work

- **Observation:** The magic is in noticing before she has to ask. Watch for subtle signs—crossed arms, rubbing her hands, or pulling sleeves over her fingers.
- **Execution:** Don't just hand her the blanket—actually wrap it around her shoulders, creating a moment of enveloping care.
- **Connection:** After placing the blanket, you might sit closer to her, adding your body warmth to the gesture without making it about you.

When to Use

This gesture works beautifully during movie nights, while reading together on the couch, or sitting outside as evening temperatures drop. It's especially powerful during transitional seasons when temperatures can be unpredictable, showing you're attuned to her changing comfort levels.

Chapter 7
Gently Tracing Patterns on Her Palm

Why It Helps

The hands contain thousands of nerve endings, making them incredibly receptive to gentle touch. When you take her hand and slowly trace patterns on her palm, you're creating a direct line of sensory connection that's both calming and stimulating. This gesture is intimate without being overtly sexual, creating a bubble of tactile connection between you.

What makes this especially powerful is the contrast between the vulnerability of an open palm and the safety of your touch upon it. It's a gesture that says: *I appreciate your openness. I'll respond with gentleness.* This combination of vulnerability and safety is the foundation of deeper intimacy.

Phrase to Say

"Your hands tell such interesting stories." OR "Did you know palm reading is just an excuse to hold someone's hand longer?"

Tips to Make It Work

- **Pacing:** Start slowly and with lighter pressure, allowing the sensitivity of her palm to adjust to your touch.
- **Attention:** Focus completely on the sensation and connection, making this moment about presence rather than conversation.
- **Creativity:** Vary your patterns—try tracing letters spelling a message, following her life lines, or creating spirals that start at the center of her palm and work outward.

When to Use

This gesture works wonderfully during quiet conversations, while watching TV together, or in moments of reconnection after time apart. It's particularly effective during pauses in conversation, creating non-verbal intimacy that often says more than words.

Chapter 8
Noticing and Complimenting a Detail in Her Outfit

Why It Helps

When you notice and comment on a specific detail of her outfit—the unique pattern on her scarf, the vintage buttons on her blouse, the particular shade of her shoes—you're demonstrating something significant: you're truly seeing her, not just looking at her. This kind of specific observation shows that you're paying attention to the choices she makes in how she presents herself to the world.

The specificity is what makes this powerful. "You look nice" is pleasant but forgettable. "The way that necklace catches the light brings out the gold flecks in your eyes" shows attentiveness and appreciation of her unique beauty and choices.

Phrase to Say

"The detail on your [specific item] is fascinating—it suits you perfectly." OR "I love how that [color/pattern/texture] captures something essential about you." (refer to tip 11 in the beginnning of the book if these don't work for you!)

Tips to Make It Work

- **Authenticity:** Only comment on what genuinely catches your eye. Women have remarkable radar for insincerity.
- **Specificity:** The more precise your observation, the more impact it has. Notice textures, colors, patterns, or how different elements work together.
- **Timing:** Offer this observation naturally, not as an obligatory greeting or automatic response.

When to Use

This gesture works wonderfully when she's made an effort for an occasion, when she's wearing something new, or when you notice her wearing something that particularly reflects her personality. It's also powerful when used to acknowledge everyday beauty, not just special-occasion appearance.

Chapter 9
Making Her Laugh with a Silly Dance

Why It Helps

In a world where men often feel pressure to appear composed and in control, the willingness to be deliberately silly creates a refreshing break from expectations. When you dance goofily —whether it's exaggerated moves to a song on the radio or a spontaneous victory dance when the pasta water finally boils —you're saying: *I'm comfortable enough with you to be ridiculous. I value your joy above my dignity.*

This gesture creates laughter, yes, but it does something even more powerful: it demonstrates emotional security. A man secure enough to look foolish for her smile is a man secure enough to be trusted with her heart.

Phrase to Say

"This is my special dance I save only for you." OR "Sometimes the only appropriate response is interpretive dance."

Tips to Make It Work

- **Commitment:** Half-hearted silly dancing is just awkward. Commit fully to the absurdity.
- **Personalisation:** Incorporate inside jokes or references unique to your relationship for extra impact.
- **Timing:** Choose moments when levity would be welcome—during cooking, cleaning, or when she seems stressed or too serious.

When to Use

This gesture is perfect for breaking tension, transitioning from work mode to home mode, or simply injecting playfulness into routine moments. It works especially well when unexpected—dancing in the kitchen while making dinner, in the laundry room while folding clothes, or as a greeting when she returns home after a long day.

Chapter 10
Whispering Something Sweet
When Others Can't Hear

Why It Helps

In the midst of a crowded room, a whispered comment creates an island of intimacy that belongs only to you two. This gesture transforms any public setting into a private moment, reminding her that regardless of who else is present, your focus remains uniquely on her. It's the conversational equivalent of a secret touch—unseen by others but deeply felt.

When you lean in close, keeping your voice low enough that only she can hear, you're creating a world within a world. The physical proximity combined with the exclusivity of your words forms a powerful connection, often leaving her with both a smile and a delicious shiver.

Phrase to Say

"I've never told anyone this, but..." OR "I can't stop noticing how everyone keeps looking at you."

Tips to Make It Work

- **Proximity:** Get close enough that your breath lightly touches her ear or neck as you speak—this sensory element amplifies your words.
- **Content:** The whisper can be sweet, funny, or slightly mischievous—but should make her feel like the most interesting person in the room.
- **Retreat:** After whispering, pull back slightly to catch her expression, creating a complete circuit of connection.

When to Use

This gesture works perfectly at social gatherings, family events, or anywhere with ambient noise that provides a reason to lean close. Use it when you want to create contrast between the public setting and your private connection.

The Art of Non-Sexual Foreplay

*"To love a person is to learn the song that is in their heart
and to sing it to them when they have forgotten."*

— Arne Garborg

The gestures in this book are, in essence, ways of singing her song back to her—reminding her of her beauty, worth, and the unique melody she brings to the world. The deepest intimacy comes not from grand gestures but from these small moments of recognition, where she feels truly seen and celebrated for exactly who she is. When you learn to notice and honour the details that make her uniquely herself, you're practising the highest form of attention—and attention, freely given, is the purest form of love.

Chapter 11
Sending Her a Thoughtful Text During the Day

Why It Helps

In the rush of daily life, a thoughtful text lands like an unexpected gift in her day. It's not just the content—it's the fact that in the midst of meetings, deadlines, and obligations, you took a moment to think of her. This gesture bridges physical separation with emotional connection, saying plainly: *You're on my mind, even when we're apart.*

What elevates this beyond routine communication is specificity and timing. A generic "thinking of you" is nice, but a text that references something unique to her day or experience shows you're carrying her world within yours. It transforms her phone from a stress-inducing device into a portal for connection.

Phrase to Say

"That song you love just came on, and now I'll be thinking about you all afternoon." OR "Just passed that café where you laughed so hard you snorted your coffee. Still one of my favourite sounds."

Tips to Make It Work

- **Personalisation:** Reference something specific—a challenge she mentioned, a memory you share, or something that made you think of her.
- **Timing:** Send it during a part of her day when she might need a boost—mid-afternoon energy dips, right before a meeting she was nervous about, or after a milestone.
- **Expectation:** Don't require a response. The best thoughtful texts come with no strings attached—they're gifts, not requests.

When to Use

This gesture works beautifully on ordinary days (not just special occasions), when you're traveling apart, or when you know she's facing a particular challenge. It's especially powerful when unexpected—on a random Tuesday when nothing special is happening, making the ordinary day a little extraordinary.

Chapter 12
Walking on the Curb Side of the Street

Why It Helps

This old-fashioned gesture carries timeless significance. By positioning yourself between her and traffic, you're symbolically placing yourself between her and potential harm. It's a subtle act of protection that operates on both practical and symbolic levels, communicating that her safety matters to you instinctively.

The beauty of this gesture lies in its understated nature—you don't announce it or draw attention to it. You simply and naturally take the position of potential risk, creating a small buffer between her and the outside world. It's protection without possession, care without control.

Phrase to Say

This gesture works best when done without verbal acknowledgment, but if she notices and comments: "Some habits are worth keeping, especially when they involve you." OR "It's just instinct when I'm with someone who matters to me."

Tips to Make It Work

- **Smoothness:** Make the positioning natural, not a dramatic manoeuvre that interrupts conversation or flow.
- **Consistency:** Do this habitually, not just on busy streets—the consistency is what makes it meaningful rather than performative.
- **Adaptability:** Be ready to switch sides when turning corners or crossing streets, maintaining your position between her and traffic seamlessly.

When to Use

This gesture applies whenever you're walking together on sidewalks beside streets. It's particularly meaningful in urban environments with busy traffic, during evening walks, or in unfamiliar neighborhoods where the protective element feels more relevant.

Chapter 13
Adjusting Her Scarf or Jacket on a Chilly Day

Why It Helps

There's something deeply caring about the small act of adjusting someone's clothing against the cold. When you gently fix her scarf to better cover her neck or button her coat's top button as the wind picks up, you're demonstrating attentiveness to her comfort and wellbeing on a fundamental level.

This gesture succeeds because it combines practical care with gentle touch in a way that doesn't intrude on her autonomy. You're not dressing her; you're fine-tuning her comfort. The message is clear: *I notice when you might be uncomfortable, and your wellbeing matters enough for me to take action.*

Phrase to Say

"Here, let me fix this for you—the wind's picking up." OR "Can't have you catching cold—you're too important to me."

Tips to Make It Work

- **Permission:** Approach this with a lightness that gives her space to accept or decline the adjustment.
- **Attention:** Focus on the garment, not her body—this keeps the gesture in the realm of care rather than control.
- **Follow-up:** After adjusting, you might ask, "Better?" showing that her comfort, not your action, is the priority.

When to Use

This gesture works beautifully during seasonal transitions when temperatures fluctuate, on evening outings as temperatures drop, or when entering or leaving buildings with different climate conditions. It's especially meaningful when she hasn't yet registered the temperature change herself —your awareness precedes her discomfort.

Chapter 14
Surprising Her with Her Favourite Snack

Why It Helps

There's something uniquely personal about food preferences. When you remember that she loves dark chocolate with sea salt, or can't resist kettle corn, or has a weakness for those specific cheese crackers, you're saying: *I've been paying attention to what brings you joy, even in small things.*

This gesture works on multiple levels: it shows memory (you remembered her preference), effort (you went out of your way to get it), and anticipation of needs (you thought about what might please her before she had to ask). It transforms a simple snack into evidence of ongoing attentiveness.

Phrase to Say

"I saw these and immediately thought of you." OR "I remembered these were your favourite—thought you might need a little pick-me-up."

Tips to Make It Work

- **Specificity:** The more specific to her unique preference, the more impact it has—not just any chocolate, but the exact type she once mentioned loving.
- **Timing:** Offer it during a natural moment, not with fanfare that might create pressure to respond dramatically.
- **Casualness:** Present it as though it were the most natural thing in the world to think of her while seeing her favourite snack—because it should be.

When to Use

This gesture works perfectly when she's had a challenging day, during long work sessions, as a surprise in her bag before a trip, or simply as an unexpected mid-week reminder that you're thinking of her. The ordinariness of the occasion often makes it more special than saving such gestures only for traditional gift-giving moments.

Chapter 15
Writing Her a Short Note or Love Letter

Why It Helps

With easy access to instant digital communication, taking the time to write something by hand carries increased significance. A handwritten note—whether it's three sentences on a Post-it or a full page in a card—creates something tangible she can return to repeatedly, making your words last beyond the moment.

What makes this gesture particularly powerful is the combination of effort, permanence, and exclusivity. Unlike texts or emails that can be sent to anyone, a handwritten note is uniquely for her. It transforms your feelings from ephemeral thoughts into something she can hold—physical evidence of your emotional investment.

Phrase to Write

"Sometimes I look at you and can't believe how lucky I am. You turn ordinary moments into memories I never want to forget." OR "The way you [specific quality] continues to amaze me. Thank you for bringing that into my life every day."

Tips to Make It Work

- **Honesty:** Write from a place of genuine feeling, not what you think a love note "should" say. Authenticity always resonates more than eloquence.
- **Specificity:** Include at least one detail that could only apply to her, making it impossible to mistake this note for something generic.
- **Placement:** Leave it where she'll find it unexpectedly —in her purse, on her pillow, tucked into a book she's reading.

When to Use

This gesture works beautifully as a random surprise on ordinary days, tucked into her luggage before a trip apart, after witnessing a moment where she impressed you, or as a quiet acknowledgment of a personal milestone that others might not recognise. While suitable for special occasions, its impact is often greater when unexpected.

NOTE: I have a book coming in June 2025 called "Easy Poetry For Good Men" that could help with this. See the resources at the back of this book for details.

Chapter 16
Taking Her Hand When Crossing the Street

Why It Helps

There's something timelessly intimate about reaching for her hand at a crosswalk. This gesture combines protection with connection, creating a moment of physical unity before you step into potential traffic. It communicates care without words: *I'm aware of our surroundings, and instinctively want to keep you close and safe.*

What makes this especially powerful is its instinctive quality. When done naturally—without overthinking—it becomes a physical expression of your protective instincts. The brief squeeze of your hand around hers creates a momentary refuge of connection in public space.

Phrase to Say

This gesture speaks for itself and often works best without words. If anything: "Let me have this hand for a moment." OR Simply a gentle "Ready?" before stepping off the curb together.

Tips to Make It Work

- **Naturalness:** Offer your hand with casual confidence —not tentatively, but not forcefully either.
- **Pressure:** A slight increase in hand pressure as you first step off the curb subtly communicates the protective aspect.
- **Release:** When appropriate after crossing, release naturally unless she maintains the connection— allowing the gesture to be about safety rather than possessiveness.

When to Use

This gesture is obviously perfect when actually crossing streets, but can extend to similar situations—navigating a crowded venue, walking through a busy parking lot, or traversing uneven terrain. The key is that it feels motivated by momentary care rather than arbitrary control.

Chapter 17
Fixing Something for Her Without Being Asked

Why It Helps

When you notice that loose doorknob she keeps struggling with or the wobbly chair she unconsciously avoids and quietly fix it without announcement or fanfare, you're communicating something vital: *I pay attention to the small frustrations in your environment, and I'm willing to address them without being prompted.*

This gesture succeeds because it combines observation with action. You've not only noticed what causes her friction, but you've taken initiative to eliminate that friction. It's care expressed through competence—solving problems she might have learned to live with but shouldn't have to.

Phrase to Say

If she notices and comments, keep it simple: "I noticed it was bothering you, so I thought I'd take care of it." OR "It was a quick fix—I just wanted to make your day a little easier."

Tips to Make It Work

- **Selectivity:** Choose issues that clearly impact her daily comfort—not projects that primarily interest you.
- **Timing:** Do this when she's not around, so it becomes a discovery rather than a performance.
- **Humility:** If thanked, accept appreciation gracefully without magnifying the effort it took.

When to Use

This gesture works best for minor but persistent irritations she's mentioned or that you've observed her working around. It's particularly meaningful when fixing something she's resigned herself to dealing with or has put off addressing due to time constraints or uncertainty about how to approach it.

Chapter 18
Watching Her Favourite Movie, Even If It's Not Your Type

Why It Helps

Few gestures demonstrate investment in someone's joy more clearly than willingly engaging with their interests, especially when they differ from your own. When you not only agree to watch her favourite film but engage with it genuinely— asking questions, noting details, remembering character names—you're saying something significant: *What matters to you matters to me because you matter to me.*

The power of this gesture lies not in passive tolerance but active engagement. Anyone can silently endure a film they don't prefer; the intimacy comes from your willing participation in her enjoyment, your desire to understand what moves her.

Phrase to Say

"I'd love to understand why this film is so special to you." OR After watching: "I can see why you connect with [specific character or theme]—that actually reminds me of you."

Tips to Make It Work

- **Attentiveness:** Put away your phone and other distractions, making it clear the film has your full attention.
- **Curiosity:** Ask thoughtful questions about her favourite scenes or characters (or players if its a sport), inviting her to share why they resonate.
- **Connection:** Look for genuine points of appreciation, even if the genre isn't your preference.

When to Use

This gesture works beautifully on quiet evenings at home, during times when she needs emotional comfort (many people rewatch favourites during stress), or as a surprise when she's mentioned wanting to see a film again. It's particularly meaningful when she knows it wouldn't be your first choice but you suggest it anyway.

NOTE: This can also translate to watching her favourite sport or TV show! Find out why she likes it so much!

Chapter 19
Pulling Out Her Chair at Dinner

Why It Helps

Some traditions endure because they continue to carry meaning. Pulling out her chair is one such gesture—timeless not because women can't seat themselves, but because it creates a moment of focused attention and care at the beginning of a shared experience.

This gesture works when performed with natural confidence rather than awkward formality. It briefly positions you in service to her comfort, setting a tone of attentiveness for the interaction to follow. The message is subtle but clear: *Your comfort matters to me. I'm here to enhance your experience, not just share space with you.*

Phrase to Say

This gesture typically works without words, but a simple: "Allow me." OR A quiet "Here you are" can complement the action naturally.

Tips to Make It Work

- **Timing:** Move smoothly to the chair as you approach the table, arriving just before she does.
- **Technique:** Pull the chair out enough that she can easily sit without awkward adjustments.
- **Follow-through:** Once she's seated, gently guide the chair forward as she sits, being attentive to her positioning.

When to Use

This gesture is obviously well-suited to restaurant dining, but can extend to any seated gathering—dinner parties, work functions, family meals, or even at home for special occasions. What makes it special isn't the formality of the setting but the consistency of your attentiveness.

Chapter 20
Warming Up Her Car on a Cold Morning

Why It Helps

There are few contrasts more stark than stepping from a warm house into a freezing car. When you quietly slip out to start her car before she leaves for work on a cold morning, you're addressing a universal discomfort—showing foresight and care in a particularly tangible way.

What makes this gesture especially meaningful is how it acknowledges the reality of her day. You're not just performing a mechanical task; you're recognising her schedule, anticipating a discomfort she would face, and taking action to eliminate it before she even experiences it. It's protection extended through time.

Phrase to Say

"Your car's ready when you are—should be warm by now." OR "Just wanted to make the start of your day a little more comfortable."

Tips to Make It Work

- **Anticipation:** Do this without being asked, ideally before she's even thinking about leaving.
- **Completion:** Don't just start the car—adjust the heat settings, perhaps even scrape ice if needed, making it truly ready for her departure.
- **Understatement:** Present this as a simple act rather than a grand gesture deserving elaborate thanks.

When to Use

This gesture obviously works during cold winter mornings, but can be adapted for various seasons—cooling the car in summer heat, for instance. It's particularly meaningful on days when she's already facing challenges—important meetings, early appointments, or stressful workdays where every additional comfort matters.

"When time is our most precious commodity, choosing to spend it noticing what would bring someone comfort or joy is a profound act of love."

These gestures might seem small when listed individually, but collectively they create a relationship environment where attention becomes a constant. Think of each gesture as a brushstroke—seemingly minor in isolation, but essential to the masterpiece you're creating together. The most beautiful relationships aren't built on grand, infrequent gestures, but on this daily artistry of noticing and responding to each other's needs, often before they're even expressed.

Chapter 21
Noticing When She Changes Her Hairstyle

Why It Helps

A woman's hair is often deeply connected to her identity and self-expression. When you notice and comment on a change in her hairstyle—whether dramatic or subtle—you're recognising something significant: you see the details of her self-presentation and value the choices she makes about her appearance.

The effectiveness of this gesture lies in its specificity. "You look nice" is forgettable; "I love how that new fringe frames your eyes" shows genuine attention. It acknowledges both her decision to make a change and your consistent awareness of her. The message is clear: *You don't blend into the background for me; I notice the evolving details of who you are.*

Phrase to Say

"Your new hairstyle really brings out the shape of your face." OR "I noticed you changed your hair—it looks fantastic on you."

Tips to Make It Work

- **Timeliness:** Comment soon after seeing the change—delayed recognition diminishes the impact significantly.
- **Detail:** Mention something specific about what you like, rather than generic approval.
- **Sincerity:** Only comment positively if you genuinely appreciate the change; inauthentic compliments are easily detected.

When to Use

This gesture works perfectly after she visits the salon, when she styles her hair differently for an occasion, or even when she simply wears it up instead of down. The key is consistent attention to these details, not just noticing dramatic changes.

Additional Note:

If she tells you she's got a hair appointment, set a reminder in your phone for 5 minutes before you see her again to look at and compliment her hair. If you're not sure what to say, try "Do you like your hair as much as last time?" Trust me, every cut is slightly different, even when it looks the same!

Chapter 22
Offering Your Coat When She's Cold

Why It Helps

Offering your coat when she shivers slightly or crosses her arms against the cold speaks to something fundamental in human connection—the willingness to accept personal discomfort to ensure her comfort. This gesture combines practical care with symbolic meaning: *Your wellbeing matters more to me than my own convenience.*

What elevates this beyond simple courtesy is attentiveness and timing. Offering before she has to ask shows you're tuned in to her physical state. The fact that you'll now be colder yourself transforms it from a mere practical solution into a meaningful sacrifice, however small.

Phrase to Say

"Here, take my coat—I run warm anyway." OR "I'd rather you be comfortable than me."

Tips to Make It Work

- **Observation:** Watch for subtle signs of cold—rubbing arms, hunching shoulders, or subtle shivering— rather than waiting for an explicit statement.
- **Insistence:** Offer sincerely enough to overcome polite resistance, but without forcing acceptance.
- **Follow-through:** Resist the urge to comment on your own discomfort afterwards—that undermines the generosity of the gesture.

When to Use

This gesture is obviously suited to unexpected temperature drops, evening outings as temperatures fall, or situations where she's underdressed for the conditions. It's particularly meaningful when the coat will genuinely help her comfort level, not just as a symbolic offering.

Chapter 23
Picking Flowers for Her from a Roadside Field

Why It Helps

There's an unmatched charm in spontaneously stopping to gather wildflowers you've spotted while travelling together. Unlike store-bought bouquets, wildflowers represent a moment of inspired appreciation—you saw beauty in your shared environment and wanted her to have a piece of it. This gesture says: *You inspire me to notice beauty, and I want to share it with you.*

The value here comes from the unexpectedness and personalisation. These aren't flowers from a scheduled delivery or obligatory occasion; they're a physical representation of a moment when you were moved to action by the combination of natural beauty and your feelings for her.

Phrase to Say

"These reminded me of you—beautiful but not trying too hard." OR "I thought these deserved to be appreciated up close, just like you."

Tips to Make It Work

- **Spontaneity:** The impromptu nature is what makes this special—don't plan it, but act on genuine impulse.
- **Presentation:** The handover should be casual rather than ceremonial—the gesture speaks for itself without grand flourishes.
- **Selection:** Choose flowers that have some unique quality—unusual colour, delicate structure, or vibrant presence—rather than gathering random weeds.

When to Use

This gesture works beautifully during countryside drives, walks through parks or natural areas, or even urban environments where wildflowers persist. The key is genuine spontaneity—stopping when you're genuinely moved by the sight, not creating artificial opportunities.

BONUS:

If you're out for a walk and see nice flowers (yes, even as a man you can appreciate the beauty of nature!) take a photo and send to her. Get close to the flower so the background is blurred for a better effect!

Chapter 24
Complimenting Her Without Focusing on Her Looks

Why It Helps

While appearance-based compliments have their place, acknowledging her intelligence, perspective, resilience, or kindness reaches a deeper level of recognition. This type of compliment says: *I see beyond the surface to who you truly are, and that person impresses me.*

The power of this gesture lies in its ability to make her feel valued for qualities she has cultivated rather than attributes she was born with or that conform to external standards. It validates her inner self—the person she has chosen to become rather than simply how she appears.

Phrase to Say

"The way you handled that difficult situation showed such emotional intelligence." OR "I'm consistently impressed by how you think about problems—you see angles no one else notices."

Tips to Make It Work

- **Specificity:** Tie your compliment to a particular situation or example you've observed, making it impossible to mistake for a generic flattery.
- **Uniqueness:** Focus on qualities that are distinctly hers—not general positive attributes anyone might have.
- **Delivery:** Offer these compliments during quiet moments where they can be properly absorbed, not rushed exchanges.

When to Use

This gesture is perfect after you've witnessed her handle a challenging situation well, during reflective conversations, or as a thoughtful observation during everyday activities. Unlike appearance compliments, these deeper recognitions often work better in private settings where she can fully receive them without self-consciousness.

Chapter 25
Taking Over a Task She's Struggling With

Why It Helps

There's a deep sense of awareness in quietly stepping in when you notice her frustration mounting with a particular task. Whether it's technology that won't cooperate, a jar that won't open, or assembly instructions that make no sense, offering help without being asked communicates keen awareness of her emotional state and a desire to ease her path.

The effectiveness of this gesture depends on execution—it must feel like support, not takeover. The message should be: *I'm here to help, not because you can't do this, but because I care about your experience and wellbeing.*

Phrase to Say

"Would you like me to take a turn with that?" OR "Sometimes a fresh perspective helps—mind if I try?"

Tips to Make It Work

- **Timing:** Offer help at the point of frustration, but before complete exasperation sets in.
- **Approach:** Frame your offer as collaboration rather than rescue—you're working together on the problem, not saving her from incompetence.
- ! **Permission:** Always ask before taking over, ensuring she maintains agency in the situation.

When to Use

This gesture works perfectly with practical challenges—technology issues, physical tasks requiring different strength, or situations where your specific skills might complement hers. It's particularly meaningful when the task is causing visible stress or interfering with what could otherwise be an enjoyable experience.

Chapter 26
Reaching for Her Hand in the Middle of a Crowd

Why It Helps

In the midst of a busy environment, reaching for her hand creates an island of connection that grounds both of you. This gesture establishes a physical link that says: *Among all these people, you're my person. I want to stay connected to you even in this crowd.*

What makes this particularly meaningful is how it creates privacy within public space. Hand-holding is both a practical way to stay together in crowds and a silent affirmation of your bond visible to others. It's subtle possession without possessiveness—an acknowledgment of connection rather than control.

Phrase to Say

This gesture often works best without words, letting the physical connection speak for itself. If anything: "Stay close to me." OR A simple "There you are" as your hands connect.

Tips to Make It Work

- **Initiation:** Extend your hand with quiet confidence—
  not grabbing for hers, but clearly inviting the
  connection.
- **Grip:** Find that perfect middle pressure—secure
  enough to feel connected, gentle enough to be
  comfortable for extended holding.
- **Adaptation:** Be mindful of her comfort in different
  situations—adjusting your grip for walking versus
  standing, loosening if her hand feels warm.

When to Use

This gesture works beautifully in crowded public spaces—
busy streets, festivals, shopping centres, or concert venues.
It's particularly meaningful in situations where it would be
easy to become physically separated, adding practical
purpose to the emotional connection.

BONUS:

If you know you get sweaty palms at times, keep a
handkerchief or tissue in your pocket and hold her hand for
short bursts, wiping your hand from time to time. She'll
appreciate the forethought of being prepared enough to want
to maintain the connection.

Chapter 27
Helping Her Put On Her Jewellery

Why It Helps

The act of helping clasp a necklace or secure an earring creates a moment of quiet service and proximity. As you stand behind her to fasten a necklace or steady your hands to help with a delicate bracelet clasp, you're engaging in a ritualised form of care that says: *I'm attentive to the details that complete you.*

This gesture combines physical closeness with focused attention on a small, precise task related to her adornment. There's something almost ceremonial about it—participating in her preparation and completion, particularly for meaningful occasions.

Phrase to Say

"Let me help you with that." OR After fastening a necklace: "Perfect—it looks beautiful on you."

Tips to Make It Work

- **Steadiness:** Move deliberately and carefully, treating her jewellery as the precious items they are.
- **Proximity:** Allow the natural closeness this task requires, but maintain a respectfulness that makes the moment about service rather than your own desire for contact.
- **Completion:** You might add a small touch—a light brush of fingers across her neck after fastening a necklace, or a gentle squeeze of her hand after helping with a bracelet.

When to Use

This gesture is perfectly suited to moments of preparation—before leaving for an evening out, getting ready for special events, or anytime she's wearing jewellery that's difficult to fasten alone. It's particularly meaningful with pieces that hold emotional significance, acknowledging their importance through your careful handling.

Chapter 28
Playing With Her Hair Absentmindedly

Why It Helps

Few sensations are as soothing as gentle fingers in your hair. When you casually stroke her hair while watching television or talking, you're creating physical comfort that generates emotional security. This seemingly unconscious touch says: *I find comfort in our physical connection even when my attention is elsewhere.*

What makes this gesture particularly effective is its organic quality. Unlike more deliberate forms of touch, this has an unplanned intimacy—the physical expression of comfort in each other's presence. It creates a feedback loop of relaxation: your touch soothes her, her relaxation deepens your connection.

Phrase to Say

This gesture typically works without words, but if she comments: "Your hair is irresistible—hope you don't mind." OR "I never realised how calming this would be for both of us."

Tips to Make It Work

- **Gentleness:** Keep your touch light and unhurried— this is about soothing, not styling.
- **Responsiveness:** Pay attention to how she reacts— some women love scalp massage, others prefer light stroking, and some might prefer you stick to the ends.
- **Naturalness:** Let this emerge organically during relaxed moments rather than as an announced intention.

When to Use

This gesture works beautifully during quiet evenings together —while watching films, reading side by side, or during conversations where you're physically close. It's particularly effective during transitions from busy activity to relaxation, helping signal a shift into more intimate, connected time.

BONUS:

Adding a gentle head massage often goes down well. Try not to pull her hair at the roots. Instead, spread your hand out with your fingers against her scalp, and make small circle movements. Then move your fingers to a new location and do it again.

Chapter 29
Letting Her Choose the Playlist During a Drive

Why It Helps

Control of the car ambiance might seem trivial, but surrendering it represents something significant: a willingness to enter her audio world. When you hand over playlist duties for a drive, you're saying: *I value your preferences and want to experience what you enjoy, even in this small domain.*

This gesture acknowledges that music creates emotional landscapes. By allowing her choices to shape the sonic environment you both inhabit, you're participating in her internal world. It demonstrates openness to her influence on your shared experience.

Phrase to Say

"I'd love to hear what you're into lately—mind being our DJ?" OR "Your music taste always surprises me in the best ways— what are we listening to today?"

Tips to Make It Work

- **Engagement:** Show genuine interest in her selections —ask about artists you don't recognise or comment on songs you particularly enjoy.
- **Receptivity:** Resist the urge to criticise or dismiss genres outside your preference—focus on experiencing rather than judging.
- **Participation:** When she plays something she clearly loves, note her enthusiasm—this is glimpse into her emotional world worth acknowledging.

When to Use

This gesture is obviously suited to car journeys, but extends to any shared environment with music—preparing dinner, relaxing at home, or working on projects together. It's particularly meaningful on longer drives where the musical landscape becomes a significant part of the shared experience.

Chapter 30
Remembering a Small Detail She Mentioned in Passing

Why It Helps

When you reference something she mentioned weeks ago—perhaps a book she wanted to read, a restaurant she was curious about, or a small preference she noted once—you demonstrate something powerful: you truly listen when she speaks. This gesture says: *Your words matter to me. I collect and treasure the details of who you are.*

The impact comes from unexpectedness. She likely assumes these passing comments evaporate after they're spoken. When you prove they don't—that they remain in your consciousness—it creates a profound sense of being valued and heard at a deep level.

Phrase to Say

"Didn't you mention wanting to try this place a few weeks ago? I thought we could go today." OR "I remembered you said green tea makes you jittery, so I got you this herbal blend instead."

Tips to Make It Work

- **Timing:** Allow enough time to pass that she wouldn't expect you to remember—the surprise enhances the impact.
- **Casualness:** Mention the remembered detail naturally, without drawing excessive attention to your remarkable memory.
- **Accuracy:** Be sure you've remembered correctly—a misremembered detail can backfire, suggesting you weren't listening carefully after all.

When to Use

This gesture works magnificently when you can take action based on the remembered detail—finding that book she mentioned, suggesting that restaurant she was curious about, or avoiding that food she said disagrees with her. The practical application proves you not only remembered but found the detail important enough to influence your decisions.

BONUS:

I use Keep notes on my phone to add little things that come up. E.g. likes white flowers, hates coconut chocolate, wants to visit the Louvre, likes lavender bath salts (ask what she likes as some women don't like lavender on their body! I also add important dates, artists and other things. This is especially handy when it's a new relationship!

The Art of Non-Sexual Foreplay

"Tenderness and kindness are not signs of weakness and despair, but manifestations of strength and resolution."
— Kahlil Gibran

The gestures in this section particularly exemplify this truth—that tenderness requires strength. It takes confidence to prioritise another's comfort, attention to notice subtle needs, and resolution to consistently show care through small actions. In a culture that often confuses dominance with masculinity, these moments of gentle attentiveness represent a more profound strength: the power to create security and connection through deliberate tenderness.

Chapter 31
Giving Her a Genuine, Lingering Compliment

Why It Helps

There's a world of difference between a passing "you look nice" and a thoughtful compliment delivered with presence and intention. When you pause to truly see her, then express specific appreciation with unhurried sincerity, you're creating a moment that transcends ordinary interaction. This deliberate recognition says: *I've paused to really see you, and what I see moves me enough to put it into words.*

The distinction lies in delivery as much as content. A lingering compliment involves full attention—a brief suspension of everything else to focus entirely on her and what you appreciate. This quality of presence transforms words into an experience of being truly seen.

Phrase to Say

"The way your whole face lights up when you talk about your work is captivating—it shows how passionate you are." OR "I've been noticing how gracefully you navigate difficult conversations. It's a rare quality, and I admire it deeply."

Tips to Make It Work

- **Presence:** Deliver the compliment with your full attention—put down your phone, pause what you're doing, and connect with your eyes.
- **Specificity:** Focus on something distinctive that reflects her unique qualities rather than generic positives anyone might possess.
- **Authenticity:** Only compliment what genuinely moves you—insincere praise is worse than no compliment at all.

When to Use

This gesture works beautifully in unexpected moments— during ordinary activities when something about her suddenly strikes you. While suitable for special occasions, its impact is often greater during everyday life, elevating routine moments into memorable connections.

Chapter 32
Adjusting Her Seatbelt or Bag Strap Thoughtfully

Why It Helps

A gentle adjustment of her seatbelt where it might be uncomfortable, or shifting a heavy bag strap that's digging into her shoulder, demonstrates a particular kind of attentiveness—noticing potential discomfort before she has to mention it. This small act of care communicates: *I'm paying attention to your physical comfort, even in ways you might not mention yourself.*

What makes this gesture particularly meaningful is how it addresses subtle discomforts that many people simply endure without comment. Your attention to these details shows remarkable attunement to her experience and a desire to improve it in tangible, immediate ways.

Phrase to Say

"Let me adjust this for you—it doesn't look comfortable." OR A simple "May I?" as you reach to make the adjustment.

Tips to Make It Work

- **Permission:** Always use a light touch and an asking gesture or comment before adjusting anything touching her body.
- **Precision:** Make the adjustment effectively, not just symbolically—actually improve the situation rather than merely calling attention to it.
- **Discretion:** Handle this matter-of-factly, without making her feel fussed over excessively.

When to Use

This gesture is perfect for car journeys (seatbelt adjustments), walks with bags or backpacks, or anytime you notice straps, tags, or accessories that might be causing discomfort. It's particularly appreciated during long journeys or outings where small discomforts can compound over time.

Chapter 33
Making Her a Meal or Snack She Loves

Why It Helps

Preparing food specifically to her taste represents one of the most fundamental forms of care. When you take the time to create something you know she enjoys—whether an elaborate meal or a simple snack prepared just how she likes it—you're saying: *I pay attention to what brings you pleasure, and I'm willing to invest time and effort to provide that experience.*

Food preparation carries primal significance in human connection. By nourishing her according to her preferences rather than just your own, you demonstrate both attentiveness to her unique tastes and willingness to adapt your efforts to her satisfaction rather than convenience.

Phrase to Say

"I made this exactly how you like it." OR "I remember you mentioned craving this—thought it might make your day a bit better."

Tips to Make It Work

- **Precision:** Pay attention to her specific preferences—not just what she likes, but exactly how she likes it prepared.
- **Presentation:** Serve it with care that shows this wasn't just about hunger, but about creating a pleasant experience.
- **Timing:** Offer food when it will be most appreciated —when she's busy, tired, or mentioned being hungry —rather than when it might interrupt her flow.

When to Use

This gesture works wonderfully after a long day, during a busy work period, when she's feeling under the weather, or simply as an unexpected pleasure on an ordinary day. It's particularly meaningful when you prepare something she's mentioned enjoying in the past, showing you both remembered and took action on that knowledge.

Chapter 34
Offering Your Arm as You Walk Together

Why It Helps

There's something elegantly connective about offering your arm as you walk together. This simple gesture creates a physical link that's both supportive and dignified, allowing closeness while maintaining a certain grace. It communicates: *We belong together, and I take pleasure in our public connection.*

Unlike hand-holding, which tends to be casual, or arm-around-the-waist, which is more possessive, the offered arm carries a distinctive blend of respect and connection. It suggests both protection and partnership—a walking embodiment of being separately whole but choosing connection.

Phrase to Say

This gesture typically needs no words—simply offer your bent arm with a slight gesture or smile. If anything, a gentle: "Shall we?" OR "May I escort you?" with a touch of playful formality.

Tips to Make It Work

- **Offering:** Present your bent arm with natural confidence—not forced or awkwardly thrust forward.
- **Positioning:** Keep your arm relaxed at a comfortable height for her to hold comfortably.
- **Pace:** Adjust your walking speed to create harmony in movement—not pulling ahead or holding back.

When to Use

This gesture shines in slightly formal settings—evening outings, events, or dressed-up occasions—but can add a touch of unexpected elegance to ordinary walks as well. It's particularly appropriate when navigating uneven terrain, walking in heels, or moving through crowded areas where staying connected is practical as well as pleasant.

Chapter 35
Pulling Her Close When It Starts to Rain

Why It Helps

There's something cinematicaly romantic about pulling her close at the first drops of rain. This instinctive sheltering gesture combines practicality with romance—yes, you're providing some cover, but more importantly, you're creating instant physical closeness in response to an environmental change. It says: *My first instinct when the world changes is to bring you closer.*

The power of this gesture lies in its instinctive quality. You don't deliberate or announce—you simply draw her toward you in a fluid, protective motion that feels like the most natural response possible to the situation.

Phrase to Say

"Come here—it's starting to rain." OR No words at all—sometimes the gesture speaks most eloquently by itself.

Tips to Make It Work

- **Smoothness:** Make the movement fluid and confident —not hesitant or awkward.
- **Closeness:** Create actual shelter with your body, whether with an arm around her shoulders or drawing her under a shared jacket.
- **Continuation:** Use the moment of closeness as a starting point—maintain the connection even after finding better shelter.

When to Use

This gesture obviously works during unexpected rain showers, but extends metaphorically to other sudden changes —a cold gust of wind, an unexpectedly chilly evening, or even moving from a quiet space to a noisy one. The key element is the instinctive drawing closer in response to environmental shift.

Chapter 36
Taking Notice of Her Favourite Perfume

Why It Helps

A woman's chosen scent is intensely personal—often selected carefully to express something about her essence or to create a specific sensory impression. When you notice and comment appreciatively on her perfume—especially identifying it by name if you know it—you're acknowledging: *I pay attention to the sensory details that make up your presence, including the ones you've deliberately chosen.*

What makes this gesture particularly meaningful is how it recognises her intentionality. Perfume is rarely accidental—it's a deliberate choice of how she wishes to be experienced by others. Your notice confirms that her choices are achieving their desired effect.

Phrase to Say

"You're wearing that perfume I love—the one that reminds me of summer evenings." OR "That scent is so distinctly you —I could recognise it anywhere."

Tips to Make It Work

- **Subtlety:** Comment in a low voice, creating intimacy around your observation.
- **Specificity:** Note something particular about how the scent works with her, not just that you noticed it.
- **Memory:** If possible, connect the scent to a specific memory or moment you share—scent and memory are powerfully linked.

When to Use

This gesture works beautifully when greeting her after time apart, during close conversations, or when you notice she's wearing a scent different from her usual choice. It's particularly appreciated as a whispered observation while in public—a private recognition in a shared space.

Chapter 37
Reading Aloud a Poem or Passage That Made You Think of Her

Why It Helps

There is remarkable intimacy in sharing words that made you think of her. When you read aloud a poem, passage, or quote that connected to her in your mind, you're offering a glimpse into both your inner thoughts and how you see her. This gesture says: *You exist in my mind even when we're apart, and I find echoes of you in unexpected places.*

This gesture is powerful because it combines discovery with recognition. You've encountered something meaningful in your separate experience, recognised its relevance to her or your relationship, and created a moment of connection by sharing it aloud—bridging your individual worlds through words.

Phrase to Say

"I came across this and immediately thought of you." OR "These words captured something about you I've always felt but couldn't express."

Tips to Make It Work

- **Selection:** Choose something that genuinely resonated rather than searching for material to impress—authenticity matters more than literary prestige.
- **Delivery:** Read at a measured pace with appropriate feeling, but without dramatic performance that might create self-consciousness.
- **Context:** Briefly explain why or how it made you think of her, creating a frame for the words themselves.

When to Use

This gesture works beautifully during quiet evenings together, as a thoughtful message shared over morning coffee, or as an unexpected moment during an ordinary day. It's particularly meaningful when the selection illuminates something you admire about her that might not be regularly acknowledged in daily conversation.

Chapter 38
Offering Her the Last Piece of Something Delicious

Why It Helps

The last piece of cake, the final slice of pizza, the remaining chocolate, the last Rolo (it's an English thing!)—these take on almost mythical significance in human interactions. When you offer her this coveted final portion without hesitation, you're engaging in a small but meaningful act of putting her pleasure before your own. It states clearly: *Your enjoyment matters more to me than my immediate satisfaction.*

What elevates this beyond basic politeness is the genuine willingness behind it. This isn't about reluctantly following social conventions, but about taking pleasure in her pleasure —finding more satisfaction in her enjoyment than you would in consuming the morsel yourself.

Phrase to Say

"The last piece is yours—I insist." OR "You should have the last one—seeing you enjoy it is better anyway."

Tips to Make It Work

- **Sincerity:** Offer without that subtle sigh or reluctant energy that undermines the generosity.
- **Insistence:** If she politely declines, offer once more—often people refuse automatically but appreciate gentle persistence.
- **Enjoyment:** Take visible pleasure in her enjoyment, reinforcing that her satisfaction was the goal.

When to Use

This gesture works in any food-sharing situation—restaurants, home meals, picnics, or snacking together. It's particularly meaningful with foods you both especially enjoy, making the sacrifice more evident and therefore more appreciative.

Chapter 39
Carrying Her Bag or Groceries Without Being Asked

Why It Helps

There's something fundamentally supportive about noticing her physical burden and quietly alleviating it. When you wordlessly take her heavy bag or grocery sacks, you're demonstrating both attentiveness and practical care. This gesture communicates: *I notice what's challenging for you and want to ease your way without being prompted.*

The impact comes from the combination of observation and initiative. You've both noticed her burden and taken action without requiring her to ask for help—eliminating the mental load of having to request assistance on top of the physical load she's carrying.

Phrase to Say

"Let me take that for you." OR Simply extend your hand toward the bag with a questioning look, letting the gesture speak for itself.

Tips to Make It Work

- **Timing:** Offer before she shows signs of strain, ideally at the moment the item is first picked up.
- **Naturalness:** Make it a fluid, expected part of your interaction rather than a conspicuous display of chivalry.
- **Respect:** If she prefers to carry something herself, respect that choice without comment—the offer itself still communicates care.

When to Use

This gesture is obviously suited to shopping trips, travel with luggage, or any situation involving carried items. It's particularly appreciated with awkward or heavy loads, during longer walking distances, or when she's also managing other things (like keeping track of children or navigating difficult terrain).

Chapter 40
Planning a Surprise Outing or Date Based on Her Interests

Why It Helps

When you plan an experience specifically tailored to her interests and preferences—perhaps a visit to an exhibition by an artist she admires, tickets to see her favourite author speak, or a trip to a place she's mentioned wanting to explore —you demonstrate profound attentiveness. This gesture says: *I pay such close attention to what matters to you that I can create experiences that will bring you joy.*

What makes this particularly powerful is the combination of listening, remembering, planning, and executing—four different forms of care layered into one gesture. You've created something that could only exist because you truly know and value her unique preferences.

Phrase to Say

"I've planned something I think you'll love—just trust me with a few hours of your time." OR "Remember when you mentioned wanting to see this? I've arranged everything."

Tips to Make It Work

- **Personalisation:** Base the plan on her actual interests, not your assumptions about what women generally enjoy.
- **Details:** Handle the logistics thoroughly—tickets, transportation, timing—so she can simply experience without managing details.
- **Flexibility:** While surprise is wonderful, be adaptable if the timing isn't right or if she needs modifications to fully enjoy the experience.

When to Use

This gesture works beautifully for birthdays or anniversaries, but carries even more impact when done for no particular occasion—transforming an ordinary weekend into something memorable. It's particularly meaningful when connected to something she's mentioned in passing, showing you were truly listening.

"At the touch of love everyone becomes a poet." — Plato

This ancient wisdom captures the essence of these gestures perfectly. When we act from genuine affection, even the most ordinary actions take on poetic qualities. You don't need to write sonnets to be poetic in your relationship—these seemingly simple acts of noticing, supporting, and appreciating create a lived poetry far more meaningful than flowery words alone. The truly poetic life exists in these small moments of genuine connection, where everyday actions become vehicles for expressing what often lies beyond language.

Chapter 41
Putting on Her Favourite Song and Inviting Her to Dance

Why It Helps

There's something intensely connecting about creating an unexpected moment of movement and music in an ordinary day. When you deliberately select a song she loves and extend your hand in invitation, you're crafting a pocket of joy that exists outside routine. This gesture says: *I remember what brings you happiness and want to create that experience spontaneously with you.*

Dancing together combines multiple forms of connection—shared rhythm, physical touch, mutual movement, and the vulnerability of potential awkwardness. It's a full-sensory experience that pulls both of you out of your heads and into your bodies and the present moment.

Phrase to Say

"This song always makes me want to dance with you." OR Simply extend your hand with a smile, letting the music speak for itself.

Tips to Make It Work

- **Setting:** Clear a small space if needed, but don't wait for perfect conditions—the spontaneity is part of the charm.
- **Confidence:** Extend the invitation with warmth and certainty—hesitation can make her feel self-conscious about accepting.
- **Adaptation:** Match the dance to both the music and her comfort level—some songs call for playful twirls, others for simple swaying together.

When to Use

This gesture works beautifully in ordinary domestic moments —while cooking dinner, during weekend mornings, or as a surprise when she returns home. It's particularly effective when used to break tension, shift energy after a stressful day, or transform a mundane evening into something memorable.

BONUS: You don't have to know how to waltz for this to work! Side stepping works, swaying works, going in circles works or if her jam is heavy metal, letting it go and rocking out also works! Do what comes natrually, is fun, and makes her forgot what she was doing and create a new memory with you instead.

Chapter 42
Tucking Her Hair Behind Her Ear During a Conversation

Why It Helps

This small, almost reflexive gesture creates a moment of gentle connection during conversation. When you carefully tuck a wayward strand of hair behind her ear, you're momentarily focused entirely on her comfort and appearance in a way that feels both protective and appreciative. It communicates: *I notice the small details of you, even in the midst of our conversation.*

What makes this particularly effective is its seamless integration into ordinary interaction. Unlike more formal or deliberate touches, this brief contact feels natural and unplanned, yet creates a spark of intimacy that can transform the entire conversation's energy.

Phrase to Say

This gesture often works best without breaking the conversational flow, but if anything: "I just wanted to see your full expression." OR A simple, soft "There" as you complete the gesture.

Tips to Make It Work

- **Gentleness:** Use the lightest touch possible—this is about delicacy, not efficiency.
- **Eye Contact:** Maintain kind eye connection through the gesture, or briefly meet her eyes as you complete it.
- **Naturalness:** Let it emerge organically when hair actually needs tucking, rather than manufacturing the opportunity.

When to Use

This gesture shines during intimate conversations, moments of focused attention on one another, or whenever her hair naturally falls forward. It's particularly effective during meaningful discussions where it serves as a physical punctuation of emotional closeness.

Chapter 43
Complimenting Her Laugh or Her Mind

Why It Helps

While physical compliments have their place, acknowledging her laugh—its unique sound, how it transforms her face, how contagious it is—or her mind—its sharpness, creativity, or insight—touches on something more essential to her identity. This gesture tells her: *I see and value parts of you that are expressions of your true self, not just your appearance.*

The impact comes from recognising aspects of her that she has developed or that express her essence, rather than features she was simply born with or that conform to conventional standards. It validates her as a complete person, not merely an aesthetic object.

Phrase to Say

"Your laugh is my favourite sound in the world—especially that genuine one where you forget to be self-conscious." OR "The way you connected those ideas just now was brilliant—your mind works in fascinating ways."

Tips to Make It Work

- **Specificity:** Avoid generic praise—point to particular qualities of her laugh or thought processes that you genuinely appreciate.
- **Timing:** Offer these observations close to when you've experienced them—right after she's laughed heartily or shared an insightful perspective.
- **Authenticity:** Only comment on what truly strikes you—manufactured compliments about these deeper qualities ring particularly hollow.

When to Use

This gesture works wonderfully after genuine moments of laughter or intellectual exchange, during reflective conversations, or when you find yourself genuinely moved by an aspect of her personality. It's particularly meaningful when offered privately, creating space for her to truly receive the recognition.

Chapter 44
Drawing Her into a Slow, Heartfelt Hug

Why It Helps

There's a world of difference between a perfunctory greeting hug and one that communicates genuine presence. When you draw her into an embrace that's unhurried, secure, and fully attentive, you create a physical sanctuary of connection. This gesture conveys: *I'm fully here with you in this moment, and there's nowhere else I need to be.*

The power lies in quality rather than duration—a truly present ten-second hug can provide more connection than minutes of distracted physical contact. The key elements are full-body engagement, relaxed breathing, and a sense of both giving and receiving comfort simultaneously.

Phrase to Say

This gesture often needs no words, but if any: "Just needed to hold you for a moment." OR A simple "Mmm" of appreciation as you embrace.

Tips to Make It Work

- **Presence:** Put down your phone, set aside distractions, and be fully in the moment of connection.
- **Pressure:** Find that perfect middle ground of embrace —secure enough to feel solid, gentle enough to be comfortable.
- **Patience:** Allow the hug to find its natural conclusion rather than cutting it short or forcing it to continue.

When to Use

This gesture works beautifully as a greeting after time apart, during moments of celebration or concern, or simply as a spontaneous expression of affection during ordinary activities. It's particularly valuable during transitions— leaving for work, returning home, before sleep—creating connection points throughout the day.

NOTE: If either of you are not big huggers, start small, ask for permission and pay attention to the comfort level. If one of you pulls away don't take it personally and don't give up. Many people who "don't like" hugs had rough childhoods so it may be a strange experience. Being present is all important. No words, just connection.

Chapter 45
Telling Her What You Admire About Her Approach to Life

Why It Helps

Beyond specific actions or qualities lies something more fundamental—her unique way of moving through the world. When you articulate what you admire about her approach to life—her resilience, her kindness to strangers, her principled decisions, her joyful outlook—you're recognising her at the most essential level. This gesture says: *I see not just what you do, but who you are and how you navigate existence.*

This form of recognition touches on identity in its deepest sense—the consistent threads that run through all her choices and interactions. By noticing and naming these patterns, you demonstrate a level of attention that goes beyond surface observation to true understanding.

Phrase to Say

"I've been thinking about how you always find the humour in difficult situations. That approach to life is something I deeply admire." OR "The way you stand up for your principles, even when it's uncomfortable—that integrity is extraordinary."

Tips to Make It Work

- **Reflection:** Take time to genuinely consider what you consistently admire before speaking—this requires thought, not just impulse.
- **Specificity:** Reference particular instances that exemplify the quality you're recognising, showing this isn't abstract praise but grounded observation.
- **Setting:** Choose a moment of genuine connection rather than offering this recognition amid distractions or in passing.

When to Use

This gesture is perfect during milestone moments—birthdays, anniversaries, achievements—but carries particular weight when offered without external prompting. It's especially meaningful after you've observed her handling a situation in a way that exemplifies her core values or approach.

Chapter 46
Taking a Moment to Thank Her for Something She Does

Why It Helps

We often take for granted the consistent actions that make our lives better—the way she always remembers to buy your favourite cereal, how she listens to your work stories, her habit of turning down your side of the bed, doing the shopping, cleaning the house, taking care of the kids. When you pause to explicitly thank her for one of these everyday gestures, you're saying: *I notice and value the ways you care for me and the family that might otherwise go unacknowledged.*

What makes this particularly meaningful is how it illuminates the invisible work of relationship—all the small considerations that create comfort and connection but rarely receive recognition. Your thanks brings these contributions into the light, validating both the action and the intention behind it.

Phrase to Say

"I just realised you always remember to [specific action]. Thank you for that consistent thoughtfulness." OR "I really appreciate how you [specific detail]—it means more to me than you might realise." - or "thank you for doing the shopping today - I know you have a lot going on and still find time to do this. I really appreciate it.

Tips to Make It Work

- **Specificity:** Thank her for something particular and concrete, not general supportiveness.
- **Freshness:** Try to notice and acknowledge specific things you haven't previously recognised rather than repeating the same appreciation.
- **Sincerity:** Express genuine gratitude rather than performative thanks—the difference is palpable.

When to Use

This gesture works beautifully in ordinary moments when you genuinely notice her contribution—when she brings you coffee just how you like it, remembers something you mentioned wanting, or handles a household task that makes your life easier. The unexpectedness of the recognition in an ordinary moment is what makes it powerful.

Chapter 47
Bringing Her a Warm Towel After a Shower or Bath

Why It Helps

There's something profoundly nurturing about anticipating the moment she steps out of the shower or bath and ensuring her comfort in that vulnerable transition. When you time a warmed towel to meet her as she emerges, you're demonstrating both thoughtfulness and practical care. This gesture says: *I'm thinking about your comfort even when you're out of sight, and I want to extend the pleasure of your relaxation.*

This gesture works on multiple levels—the practical comfort of warmth, the emotional comfort of being cared for, and the thoughtful anticipation of her needs. It transforms an ordinary daily routine into a moment of unexpected luxury and attention.

Phrase to Say

"I warmed this for you." OR Simply hold out the towel with a smile, letting the action speak for itself.

Tips to Make It Work

- **Timing:** Pay attention to her bathing patterns to anticipate when she'll be finished.
- **Warming:** Use a towel warmer if you have one, or briefly tumble the towel in a dryer, or even hold it against a radiator—the method matters less than the result. Ironing it also works.
- **Presentation:** Hold it open for her to step into, creating a cocoon of warmth rather than simply handing it over.

When to Use

This gesture is obviously suited to her shower or bath time, but carries particular impact when she's had a long day, during cold weather, or when she's taking time for self-care. The contrast between the vulnerable moment of emerging from water and the immediate comfort you provide makes this especially appreciated.

Chapter 48
Laughing at Her Jokes, Even the Silly Ones

Why It Helps

Shared humour creates powerful bonds, but being the one who initiates jokes can feel vulnerable. When you genuinely laugh at her attempts at humour—especially the silly, slightly awkward ones that might not objectively be comedic masterpieces—you're offering a particular kind of validation. This response communicates: *I enjoy your unique perspective and expression, even when it's imperfect.*

What makes this especially meaningful is how it creates a safe space for her authentic expression. Your consistent, warm response to her humour—whether brilliant or groan-worthy —encourages her to be more fully herself, without self-censoring or performing.

Phrase to Say

After laughing: "Your sense of humour is one of my favourite things about you." OR "That's exactly the kind of ridiculous joke I needed today."

Tips to Make It Work

- **Authenticity:** Find something genuinely amusing about even her less successful jokes—the attempt itself, her delivery, or her pleased expression in the telling.
- **Engagement:** Build on her humour occasionally—add to the joke, reference it later, or create running gags from particularly memorable ones.
- **Appreciation:** Let your enjoyment show physically— not just polite chuckles, but full engagement with her comedic offerings.

When to Use

This gesture is perfect anytime she makes a joke, obviously, but carries particular weight when she tries something new, takes a risk with edgier humour, or seems slightly self-conscious about her attempt. Your warm reception in these vulnerable moments builds significant trust.

Chapter 49
Sitting Close Enough for Your Knees to Touch

Why It Helps

Physical closeness doesn't always need to be dramatic to be meaningful. The subtle contact of knees touching while sitting together—at dinner, on a sofa, at a gathering—creates a point of physical connection that's both casual and intimate. This positioning says: *I want to maintain contact with you, even in this subtle way, while we engage with the world.*

The power of this gesture lies in its seeming casualness that actually requires intention. You've chosen to sit near enough for contact, maintaining a physical thread of connection even while engaged in conversation, dining, or socialising. It creates a private physical dialogue alongside whatever else is happening.

Phrase to Say

This gesture typically needs no verbal acknowledgment—the physical connection speaks for itself. You might occasionally: Give her knee a gentle squeeze during a relevant moment in conversation. OR Briefly rest your hand where your knees touch, acknowledging the connection.

Tips to Make It Work

- **Naturalness:** Position yourself close without making an obvious production of it—this should feel like a natural desire for proximity.
- **Awareness:** Be conscious of the contact rather than accidental—this intentionality is what transforms proximity into connection.
- **Responsiveness:** Notice whether she maintains the connection or subtly pulls away, respecting her preference for physical boundary in that moment.

When to Use

This gesture works beautifully in social settings where more overt affection might feel out of place, during meals at restaurants, while watching performances, or during conversations with others. It's particularly effective as a grounding point of connection in environments where your attention might otherwise seem divided.

Chapter 50
Gifting Her a Small Token for No Special Reason

Why It Helps

There's something uniquely touching about receiving a small, thoughtful gift on an ordinary Thursday. When you present her with something meaningful but modest—a book by an author she mentioned, a scarf in her favourite colour, a special ingredient for a recipe she wants to try—without any calendar-dictated occasion, you're saying: *I think of you and what would bring you joy even when social convention doesn't prompt me to.*

What distinguishes this from obligatory gift-giving is its spontaneity and specificity. It's not about the monetary value but about the attention behind the selection—a tangible proof that you actively consider what would please her, even in the midst of ordinary life.

Phrase to Say

"I saw this and immediately thought of you." OR "This isn't for any special occasion—just because it made me think of you."

Tips to Make It Work

- **Personalisation:** Choose something that reflects her specific interests or preferences, not generic "woman gifts."
- **Presentation:** Keep it casual and unannounced—the surprise element adds to the pleasure.
- **Expectation:** Make clear this is simply an expression of thought, not creating obligation for reciprocation.

When to Use

This gesture works perfectly on completely ordinary days—random weekdays when nothing special is happening. It's particularly effective when connected to something she's recently mentioned wanting or enjoying, showing you're actively listening and remembering even passing comments.

The Art of Non-Sexual Foreplay

"We can only be said to be alive in those moments when our
hearts are conscious of our treasures." — Thornton
Wilder

Reaching the midpoint of our journey through these gestures, this
quote captures their essential purpose — to cultivate consciousness of
the treasure that is your relationship. Each small action serves as a
moment of wakefulness, pulling you out of the sleepwalking that
relationships can sometimes become. These aren't merely techniques
for pleasing her, but practices for keeping yourself fully present to
the wonder of her presence in your life. The true gift of these
gestures may be how they transform not just her experience of being
loved, but your experience of loving — making you more alive to the
extraordinary privilege of caring for another human heart.

Chapter 51
Turning Off Distractions to Focus on Her Completely

Why It Helps

With constant digital intrusion, the deliberate act of putting away your phone, closing your laptop, turning off the television, and focusing your complete attention on her creates a rare space of undivided presence. This conscious choice communicates: *Nothing in this moment is more important or interesting to me than you are.*

The power of this gesture lies in its increasing rarity. When most interactions are fragmented by notifications, alerts, and divided attention, the gift of your complete focus becomes almost radical. It creates a bubble of connection where she is truly the centre of your awareness—a form of regard that has become increasingly precious.

Phrase to Say

"I want to be fully present for this conversation." OR Actions speak loudest here—simply power down or put away devices without comment, letting the gesture itself communicate your intention.

Tips to Make It Work

- **Completeness:** Don't just silence your phone—put it completely away, preferably in another room or turned off entirely.
- **Body Language:** Position yourself to face her directly, with open posture that physically expresses receptivity and attention.
- **Patience:** Allow natural silences without reaching for distraction—these pauses are often where deeper connection emerges.

When to Use

This gesture is valuable during any significant conversation, but carries particular impact during ordinary exchanges that might otherwise seem too mundane for such focused attention. It's especially powerful when she's sharing something personal, uncertain, or emotionally complex—situations where your complete presence creates safety for vulnerability.

BONUS: Try this when you're eating, watching tv or even out for a walk. Then reflect at the end how peaceful it was without all the pings and buzzes!

Chapter 52
Waking Her with Kind Words or a Gentle Touch

Why It Helps

How we wake up colours the entire day that follows. When you deliberately create a gentle transition from sleep to wakefulness—a soft touch on her shoulder, a whispered good morning, a light kiss on her forehead—you're shaping that critical transition with care. This mindful awakening says: *Even this ordinary daily moment deserves tenderness and attention.*

This gesture is powerful because it acknowledges vulnerability. Sleep is perhaps our most defenceless state, and the transition to wakefulness can be jarring when done abruptly. Your gentle approach honours this vulnerability and creates a buffer of care between unconsciousness and the demands of the day.

Phrase to Say

"Good morning, beautiful. The day is waiting for you." OR A simple, softly spoken "Hey there" with a warm smile as her eyes open.

Tips to Make It Work

- **Gentleness:** Begin with the lightest touch or softest voice, allowing a gradual transition rather than sudden alertness.
- **Patience:** Give her body and mind time to adjust—don't immediately launch into conversation or questions.
- **Warmth:** Ensure your energy is calm and positive, setting a peaceful tone for the day's beginning.

When to Use

This gesture is obviously suited to mornings when you're both waking naturally, but extends to other awakening moments—after a nap, when she's dozed off in the car, or when you need to wake her for a planned activity. It's particularly meaningful on days you know she faces challenges, providing a foundation of care before difficulties arise.

BONUS: Note, this only works if you're prepared NOT to intiate sex: As she wakes, rub her back, legs, and arms in a semi firm way. It's a great way to bring blood to the muscles and slightly energising. The fact that you do this without trying to jump her shows control, intent and greater connection than doing it for self gain! (and who knows, maybe one day she'll want to take it further, but don't make that the goal!!)

Chapter 53
Holding Her Face Gently with Both Hands During a Conversation

Why It Helps

Few gestures create more immediate intimacy than holding her face gently between your palms during a significant conversation. This rare form of touch establishes a particular kind of connection—direct, intentional, and impossible to misinterpret. It says simply and powerfully: *I want nothing between us right now—no distractions, no barriers, no distance.*

What makes this gesture so potent is its combination of tenderness and intensity. The hands framing her face create a visual focus that matches the conversational focus—her expressions become your entire world in that moment, and she can feel that complete attention physically as well as emotionally.

Phrase to Say

"I want to see you clearly while we talk about this." OR Sometimes the gesture needs no words at all—the touch itself communicates everything necessary.

Tips to Make It Work

- **Approach:** Move slowly and with clear intention, allowing her to anticipate and welcome the contact.
- **Pressure:** Use the lightest effective touch—just enough pressure to provide connection without restriction.
- **Positioning:** Hold at a comfortable angle that allows your eyes to meet naturally without strain.

When to Use

This gesture is suited to moments of significant emotional exchange—expressions of love, important relationship discussions, or times of needed reassurance. It's particularly powerful when making promises, sharing vulnerable feelings, or during reconciliation after conflict.

NOTE: If you're partner has been in an abusive past relationship this can trigger emotions so read the room, her reactions and eyes! Switch to gesture 44 - giving a heartfelt hug!

Chapter 54
Brushing Your Lips Across Her Temple

Why It Helps

The temple—that vulnerable area where skin is thin and pulse is often visible—offers a unique space for affectionate connection. When you gently brush your lips across this spot, you're creating a form of contact that is simultaneously protective and appreciative. This gesture whispers: *I cherish even the most delicate aspects of your being.*

What distinguishes this from other forms of kissing is its placement and lightness. Not quite a kiss on the cheek (which can feel familial) nor a kiss on the lips (which often carries romantic/sexual expectations), this temple connection occupies a special territory of affection that feels both protective and reverent.

Phrase to Say

This gesture typically needs no words—the touch speaks eloquently on its own. If anything, perhaps: A simple "Mmm" of appreciation. OR A whispered "Hello there" if it's a greeting touch.

Tips to Make It Work

- **Lightness:** Keep the contact feather-light—more a brush of lips than a planted kiss.
- **Duration:** Let it linger just slightly longer than a perfunctory peck, but briefer than would feel invasive.
- **Context:** Often works best as a greeting, parting, or passing gesture rather than during seated conversation.
- **Caution:** Pay attention to her reactions and don't get offended! If there are things you try that she doesn't like or reacts in a strange way, either go back to the top 11 tips at the beginning of the book or talk about it without being upset that she's not receiving your good intention the way you want or expect her to! Just saying!

When to Use

This gesture works beautifully as you pass each other in domestic settings, as a greeting when reuniting after time apart, or as a nonverbal acknowledgment during activity when conversation might interrupt flow. It's particularly effective as a way to establish connection without demanding attention or response.

Chapter 55
Running Your Fingers Through Her Hair Slowly

Why It Helps

There's something primally soothing about fingers moving gently through hair. When you take the time to run your fingers slowly from her scalp to the ends of her hair, you're engaging in a form of touch that is simultaneously relaxing and awakening. This caress communicates: *I want to provide both pleasure and comfort through my touch.*

The effectiveness of this gesture comes from its dual nature—it's both nurturing and appreciative. The scalp contains thousands of nerve endings, making this a particularly sensitive area for touch, while the careful attention to her hair acknowledges this extension of herself that many women invest significant care in maintaining.

Phrase to Say

"Your hair feels amazing." OR "I hope this feels as good for you as it does for me." or… say nothing!!!

Tips to Make It Work

- **Technique:** Start at the scalp with gentle pressure and move outward toward the ends, avoiding pulls or tangles.
- **Variation:** Alternate between lightly scratching the scalp and smoothly running fingers through the length.
- **Attention:** Notice her responses—some women prefer scalp focus, others enjoy the full-length stroke, and preferences may change with different hairstyles.

When to Use

This gesture is perfect during quiet moments together—while watching a film, during conversation, or as she rests against you. It's particularly appreciated after she's had a stressful day, when she's mentioned headache or tension, or as part of helping her unwind before sleep.

Chapter 56
Gently Kissing Her Hand and Holding It

Why It Helps

There's something timelessly romantic about bringing her hand to your lips. This gesture bridges centuries of courtship tradition with genuine present-moment connection in a way that feels both classic and freshly intimate. The kiss followed by continued holding communicates: *I honour this part of you that creates, expresses, and connects with the world.*

What elevates this beyond mere performance is the quality of attention you bring to it. When done with authentic appreciation rather than theatrical flourish, this gesture acknowledges the expressiveness and capability of her hands while creating a lingering physical connection that continues after the kiss itself.

Phrase to Say

This gesture often works best with no words at all, letting the action speak for itself. If anything, perhaps a quiet: "I've been wanting to do that." OR "Your hands are remarkable."

Tips to Make It Work

- **Approach:** Take her hand gently, making the movement deliberate enough to allow her to anticipate the gesture.
- **Contact:** Let your lips linger just long enough to make it more than perfunctory, typically on the back of the hand or knuckles.
- **Continuation:** Don't immediately release after the kiss—maintain gentle hold of her hand as you lower it, creating continuity of connection.

When to Use

This gesture works beautifully in moments of appreciation, during significant conversations, or as a greeting or parting gesture on special occasions. It can feel particularly meaningful when acknowledging her accomplishment with something created by her hands, or as a wordless expression of gratitude or admiration by kissing the tools she used to create something.

Chapter 57
Massaging Her Shoulders After a Long Day

Why It Helps

The shoulders often bear the physical manifestation of stress —tightening and rising toward the ears during challenging days. When you take time to massage this area with both skill and care, you're addressing a universal human experience of tension while providing tangible relief. This attentive touch says: *I notice your physical strain and want to actively ease your burden.*

The power of this gesture comes from its direct physical benefit combined with emotional care. You're not just symbolically acknowledging her stress—you're taking concrete action to relieve it, creating immediate improvement in her physical comfort while demonstrating your willingness to be actively involved in her wellbeing.

Phrase to Say

"You're carrying a lot of tension here—let me help with that." OR "Just relax for a few minutes—I've got this."

Tips to Make It Work

- **Technique:** Focus on the trapezius muscle with firm but gentle pressure, using thumbs to work the muscle while supporting with your fingers.
- **Responsiveness:** Pay attention to her reactions, adjusting pressure based on her verbal and nonverbal feedback.
- **Duration:** Continue long enough to make a difference —at least several minutes—rather than a token 30-second gesture.

When to Use

This gesture is perfectly suited to evenings after work, particularly after she's mentioned a stressful day, when you notice her physically tensing or shifting shoulders uncomfortably, or as part of a transition from workday to relaxation time. It's especially appreciated when offered without prompting, showing you've noticed her need before she had to express it.

Chapter 58
Letting Your Fingers Trace the Line of Her Jaw

Why It Helps

The jawline represents one of the most distinctive features of an individual face—a literal outline of uniqueness. When you slowly trace this contour with a gentle fingertip, you're acknowledging her specific beauty in a deeply personal way. This appreciative touch communicates: *I see and value the unique shape and structure that makes you distinctively you.*

This gesture creates intimacy through its focused appreciation. Unlike more general caresses, this specific attention to her facial structure demonstrates close observation and deliberate recognition. It's a form of visual-turned-tactile admiration that makes her facial identity the subject of explicit appreciation.

Phrase to Say

"You have such a beautiful profile." OR "I love the line from here to here," as your finger traces the path.

Tips to Make It Work

- **Lightness:** Use the barest pressure—this is about appreciation through touch, not manipulation of the face.
- **Pace:** Move slowly enough that the gesture feels deliberate and appreciative rather than casual or rushed.
- **Approach:** Begin at the ear or chin and follow the natural contour in one fluid movement.

When to Use

This gesture works beautifully during quiet moments of closeness—sitting together in conversation, lying facing one another, or during a natural pause in activity. It's particularly effective in moments when her profile is highlighted—by sunset light through a window, when she's looking away in thought, or when you find yourself simply appreciating her features.

Chapter 59
Drawing Small Shapes or Words on Her Back with Your Finger

Why It Helps

There's something delightfully intimate about using her back as a canvas for invisible writing or drawing. This playful touch creates a private game of connection—a secret language of sensation between just the two of you. The light tracing communicates: *We have our own special form of communication that belongs only to us.*

The charm of this gesture lies in its combination of physical pleasure and mental engagement. The gentle stimulation of nerve endings creates physical enjoyment, while the guessing element engages her mind, creating a multi-level form of connection that's both sensual and playful.

Phrase to Say

"Let's see if you can guess what I'm writing." OR "This is just between you and my fingertips."

Tips to Make It Work

- **Clarity:** Make your movements defined enough to be potentially decipherable—not so light that they become merely ticklish sensation.
- **Content:** Mix specific words with simple shapes or patterns, creating variety in what she's trying to interpret.
- **Engagement:** Encourage her guesses, creating a back-and-forth game rather than one-sided activity.

When to Use

This gesture works wonderfully during relaxed physical proximity—while watching television together, during quiet evening wind-down, or as morning play before rising. It's particularly effective when you have unhurried time to develop the interaction beyond a brief touch into a genuine exchange. It also works well when you're stuck in a queue and helps pass the time in a fun way.

Chapter 60
Leaning In to Softly Inhale Her Scent

Why It Helps

Scent forms one of our most primal connections to memory and emotion. When you deliberately lean close to inhale her natural fragrance—the scent of her hair, her neck, her skin—you're engaging with her essential identity in a deeply instinctive way. This appreciative awareness communicates: *I know you at a level beyond words or vision—I recognise and value your most elemental self.*

What makes this gesture particularly powerful is its connection to our most animalistic sensory system combined with very human restraint and appreciation. Unlike other senses, scent bypasses cognitive filtering, creating direct emotional response—yet you're approaching this powerful connection with deliberate gentleness and respect.

Phrase to Say

"You always smell incredible." OR utter a simple appreciative "Mmm" as you breathe in.

Tips to Make It Work

- **Subtlety:** Keep the inhalation gentle and appreciative rather than exaggerated or theatrical.
- **Proximity:** Come close enough to truly experience her scent, but without invading her space in a way that might feel uncomfortable.
- **Specificity:** Occasionally mention what you appreciate about her particular scent—its warmth, sweetness, or uniquely comforting quality.

When to Use

This gesture works beautifully during embraces, while standing close in greeting or farewell, or during moments of physical proximity. It's particularly meaningful when she's wearing only her natural scent rather than perfume, acknowledging the essence of her rather than an applied fragrance.

*"The real voyage of discovery consists not in seeking new
landscapes, but in having new eyes."* — Marcel Proust

*As we continue exploring these gestures, Proust's insight becomes
increasingly relevant. The most profound connection doesn't come
from grand new experiences, but from learning to truly see what's
already before you. Each gesture in this section involves a deliberate
shift in perception — choosing to notice her jawline's elegant curve,
the tension in her shoulders, the unique scent that is hers alone. The
art of non-sexual foreplay is largely the art of renewed vision —
seeing her again and again as if for the first time, with eyes that
continue to discover rather than merely recognise. This continual
rediscovery keeps desire and appreciation alive far beyond the initial
stages of attraction.*

Chapter 61
Resting Your Forehead Against Hers in a Quiet Moment

Why It Helps

There's something profoundly connecting about the simple act of resting your forehead against hers. This gesture creates both literal and symbolic alignment—a physical meeting of minds that communicates wordless understanding. The shared point of contact says: *I am with you completely in this moment, our thoughts and breath intermingling in perfect proximity.*

What makes this gesture particularly powerful is its vulnerable symmetry. Both of you are equally open, equally close, with no one leading or following. It creates a moment of perfect balance—two people choosing the same stillness, the same connection, simultaneously.

Phrase to Say

This gesture often needs no words at all—the physical connection speaks eloquently on its own. If anything, perhaps a whispered: "Just us." OR "Here we are."

Tips to Make It Work

- **Approach:** Move slowly into this position, allowing her to meet you halfway rather than pressing forward into her space.
- **Pressure:** Find that perfect balance point where connection is maintained without either of you bearing weight uncomfortably.
- **Breathing:** Be conscious of your breath—neither holding it nor overwhelming her with its force, simply sharing the same air in calm rhythm.

When to Use

This gesture creates profound connection during moments of emotional significance—after saying "I love you," during challenging conversations where you want to affirm connection despite difficulty, or celebrating moments of shared joy. It's particularly meaningful when words seem insufficient or when you want to emphasise unity beyond verbal expression.

Chapter 62
Running a Bath with Salts for Her After a Long Day

Why It Helps

There's something nurturing about preparing a bath for another person's comfort and renewal. When you take the time to run a bath, adding salts or oils, adjusting the temperature to perfection, perhaps arranging towels and a candle or three nearby, you're creating a sanctuary of care. This thoughtful gesture says: *I see your weariness and want to actively create space for your restoration, not just acknowledge it.*

What makes this gesture particularly meaningful is its extended nature. Unlike momentary touches, this creates an experience that unfolds over time—from the initial invitation to the aftermath of relaxation. You're not just offering a pleasant sensation but crafting an entire interlude of comfort in her day that continues working its magic even in your absence.

Phrase to Say

"I've run a bath for you—everything's ready when you are."

OR "You deserve some time to yourself. The bath is ready with those salts you love."

Tips to Make It Work

- **Attention:** Note her preferences for temperature, scents, and additions like salts or oils, making this truly personalised care rather than generic pampering.
- **Setup:** Consider the full experience—perhaps a folded towel within reach, a place for a book or drink, dimmed lighting or candles if she enjoys them.
- **Space:** After preparing everything, give her the gift of privacy unless she specifically invites you to stay— this is about her rejuvenation, not your presence.

When to Use

This gesture creates beautiful support after particularly demanding days, when she's mentioned feeling physically tense or depleted, during times of emotional challenge, or simply as an unexpected gift on an ordinary evening. It's particularly powerful when offered without her having to ask —noticing her need for restoration before she has to express it.

Chapter 63
Tucking Her Into Bed When She's Tired

Why It Helps

There's something profoundly nurturing about the act of literally tucking someone into bed—arranging covers, adjusting pillows, creating a cocoon of comfort around them. When you take time to settle her into rest this way, you're providing a form of care that harkens back to our most fundamental experiences of being tended to. This attentive gesture says: *I want to be the one who ensures your comfort even as you drift into unconsciousness.*

The significance of this gesture lies in its representation of safety at our most vulnerable state. Sleep requires complete surrender of consciousness and control—by creating a deliberate ritual around this transition, you're symbolically promising protection during her most defenseless hours.

Phrase to Say

"Let me make sure you're comfortable." OR "Rest well—I'll be here when you wake up."

Tips to Make It Work

- **Attentiveness:** Adjust covers to her preferred arrangement—some prefer weight and snugness, others prefer looser draping.
- **Thoughtfulness:** Consider room temperature, light levels, and sound—adjusting the environment to her optimal sleep conditions.
- **Affection:** Include a gentle concluding gesture—a kiss on the forehead, a stroke of her hair, or a light touch on her shoulder.

When to Use

This gesture is obviously suited to bedtime, but carries particular meaning when she's especially tired, feeling unwell, or after a challenging day. It's also powerfully comforting when she's falling asleep before you, creating security as she drifts off while you remain awake.

BONUS: If she falls asleep on the couch, carry her to the bedroom instead of waking her. Don't hurt yourself!! Or, if she's comfy where she is, bring a blanket and pillow to make sure she's comfy. Think about her welfare too. If you know her back hurts after sleeping on the sofa, it's still better to wake her and get her to bed!

Chapter 64
Sliding Your Fingers Down Her Arm Until You Reach Her Hand

Why It Helps

There's a particular magic in the journey from casual touch to deliberate connection. When you slowly trace your fingers from her shoulder or upper arm all the way down to her hand, eventually intertwining your fingers with hers, you're creating a narrative of intentional connection. This progressive touch says: *I'm deliberately choosing to connect with you, not just incidentally making contact.*

What makes this gesture especially effective is its combination of sensation and destination. The trail of touch along the arm creates pleasurable awareness of the entire limb, while the final arrival at hand-holding establishes a specific, mutual connection point—a journey that concludes in deliberate joining.

Phrase to Say

This gesture often works best without words, letting the progressive touch speak for itself. If anything, perhaps: A soft

"There you are" when your fingers reach hers. OR "I've been wanting to hold your hand," as your fingers intertwine.

Tips to Make It Work

- **Pace:** Move slowly enough for the journey to register as intentional rather than casually brushing past.
- **Pressure:** Keep your touch light but definite—firm enough to be clearly deliberate, gentle enough to create pleasant sensation.
- **Connection:** When you reach her hand, create a natural transition to intertwined fingers or palm-to-palm contact rather than simply stopping the motion.

When to Use

This gesture works beautifully when shifting from sitting near each other to wanting more direct connection, during conversations where you want to emphasise agreement or solidarity, or as a way of initiating physical closeness after a period of separate activities. It's particularly effective as a non-verbal way of creating connection without interrupting the flow of whatever else is happening.

Chapter 65
Placing a Soft Kiss Just Below Her Ear

Why It Helps

The area just below the ear represents one of the body's most sensitively receptive zones—rich with nerve endings and rarely touched in casual interaction. When you place a gentle kiss in this intimate location, you're acknowledging her physical sensitivity in a way that is both respectful and appreciative. This deliberate touch communicates: *I know the geography of what brings you pleasure, and I approach it with both desire and restraint.*

What distinguishes this gesture is how it honours the balance between intensity and gentleness. The location carries inherent intimacy that could easily become overwhelming if approached too forcefully, but when contacted with appropriate lightness, creates a moment of distinctive physical pleasure without crossing boundaries into explicitly sexual territory (unless you both want it to of course!).

Phrase to Say

This gesture typically needs no verbal accompaniment—the sensation itself communicates everything necessary. If anything, perhaps: A soft "Mmm" of appreciation. OR A whispered "You smell wonderful here."

Tips to Make It Work

- **Approach:** Move with unhurried deliberateness that allows her to anticipate the contact.
- **Pressure:** Keep the kiss feather-light—this area responds more to gentle attention than firm contact.
- **Duration:** Allow the moment to be brief but not rushed—lingering just long enough to register as intentional rather than incidental.

When to Use

This gesture creates meaningful connection during embraces, while passing behind her, or during moments of already established physical closeness. It's particularly effective as a greeting or farewell gesture that distinguishes your touch from ordinary social contact, creating a moment of intimate recognition amid routine interaction.

Chapter 66
Wrapping Her in Your Arms from Behind and Swaying Gently

Why It Helps

The back-to-front embrace creates a unique combination of security and freedom. When you wrap your arms around her from behind and initiate a gentle swaying motion, you're simultaneously holding her close while allowing her to look outward—contained but not confined. This enveloping gesture says: *I want to hold you close and move in harmony with you, while still allowing you to face the world.*

What makes this particularly effective is how it combines physical support with shared movement. The embrace itself offers protection and connection, while the slow swaying introduces a subtle dance-like quality that transforms static holding into dynamic togetherness—two bodies finding common rhythm without need for words or direction.

Phrase to Say

This gesture often works beautifully without words, letting the physical connection speak for itself. If anything, perhaps:

"I love holding you like this." OR A hummed fragment of music that matches your swaying rhythm.

Tips to Make It Work

- **Height Adaptation:** Adjust your positioning based on height differences—you might need to bend slightly or straighten to create the most comfortable alignment.
- **Arm Placement:** Wrap your arms around her waist or just below her ribcage, finding the position that feels most natural for both your bodies.
- **Rhythm:** Keep the swaying gentle and slow—this isn't about dramatic movement but subtle, shared motion that becomes almost meditative.

When to Use

This gesture creates beautiful connection while cooking together, looking out at a view, watching sunset, or during quiet moments at home. It's particularly wonderful during music, where your swaying can naturally align with the rhythm without becoming formal dancing. The key is finding moments where the embrace feels like a natural extension of shared presence rather than an interruption.

Chapter 67
Lifting Her Chin to Meet Your Gaze

Why It Helps

The gentle guidance of your finger beneath her chin, lifting her face to meet your gaze, creates a particular quality of visual connection. This deliberate alignment communicates multiple layers: encouragement when she's hesitant, appreciation of her features, and desire for complete eye contact. The gesture says: *I want to see you fully, and I want you to see that I'm seeing you.*

What makes this especially meaningful is how it combines gentle direction with profound respect. You're not forcing eye contact but inviting it—creating the physical conditions for deeper connection while still honouring her agency in accepting that invitation. It acknowledges both her occasional hesitancy and your desire for her openness.

Phrase to Say

"I want to see those eyes." OR "Let me see you," spoken softly as you lift her chin.

Tips to Make It Work

- **Gentleness:** Use the lightest touch possible with a single finger under her chin—this is guidance, not manipulation.
- **Timing:** Reserve this gesture for moments when she seems to be looking down from shyness or uncertainty, not when she's deliberately avoiding eye contact during conflict.
- **Connection:** Once your eyes meet, maintain the connection long enough to establish real connection—this completes the gesture's purpose.

When to Use

This gesture is particularly powerful when she's feeling insecure, after giving her a compliment she's shyly receiving, when she's sharing something vulnerable, or during intimate conversations where deeper connection is appropriate. It's especially meaningful in moments of reconciliation or renewed appreciation, symbolically bringing her back into full presence with you.

Chapter 68

Stroking Her Cheek with the Back of Your Fingers

Why It Helps

The cheek represents one of the most expressively human parts of the face—where emotion shows in flushing, where tears fall, where smiles create their distinctive shape. When you stroke this expressive canvas with the back of your fingers rather than the palm, you're employing a particularly gentle, almost reverent form of touch. This delicate contact says: *I approach the most expressive parts of you with both appreciation and care.*

Using the back of the fingers creates a distinction from utilitarian touch. Unlike the palm, which we use for functional grasping and manipulation, the back of the hand rarely serves practical purposes—making this a form of contact that exists purely for connection and appreciation, not function.

Phrase to Say

"Your skin is so soft here." OR This gesture often needs no

words at all—the touch itself communicates everything necessary.

Tips to Make It Work

- **Direction:** Move your knuckles gently from her temple toward her jaw in a fluid, unhurried motion.
- **Pressure:** Keep the contact feather-light—just enough to be distinctly felt without pressing into the skin.
- **Focus:** Maintain eye contact during this gesture when possible, creating dual connection through touch and sight.

When to Use

This gesture creates beautiful connection during quiet conversations, moments of appreciation, or transitional times like greeting or parting. It's particularly meaningful after she's been emotionally expressive—whether through laughter, tears, or passionate discussion—acknowledging the emotional landscape that shows itself on this expressive feature.

Chapter 69
Gently Holding Her Ankle as She Rests Her Feet on Your Lap

Why It Helps

There's something uniquely trusting about allowing someone to hold your feet—these utilitarian body parts we often hide or keep literally on the ground. When you create space for her feet on your lap and then gently encircle her ankle with your hand, you're acknowledging this trust and responding with supportive touch. This gesture communicates: *I welcome even the parts of you that aren't conventionally highlighted, and find connection in supporting your complete comfort.*

The significance of this gesture lies in its combination of service and intimate casualness. You're both providing physical support and maintaining connected touch in an area that's often overlooked for its connective potential. It creates comfort that's simultaneously practical and emotionally affirming.

Phrase to Say

"Rest here as long as you'd like." OR "I love these moments of simple connection."

Tips to Make It Work

- **Position:** Create a comfortable surface on your lap—perhaps with a cushion if you'll be sitting this way for an extended time.
- **Grip:** Hold her ankle lightly but securely, wrapping your fingers around in a way that feels supportive rather than restrictive.
- **Attention:** Even while engaging in other activities (watching a film, reading, conversing), maintain awareness of your touch—occasional gentle squeezes or thumb movements show continued attention.

When to Use

This gesture creates wonderful connection during relaxed evenings at home, while watching television, during casual conversations on the sofa, or in any setting where extended comfortable positioning is possible. It's particularly appreciated after she's been on her feet for long periods, creating relief alongside connection.

Chapter 70
Running Your Hand Along the Curve of Her Waist

Why It Helps

The waist represents one of the most distinctively feminine contours—a curve that defines the transition between torso and hips. When you mindfully run your hand along this silhouette, you're acknowledging her unique physical form with appreciation. This attentive touch says: *I see and value the distinctive shape that is uniquely yours.*

What makes this gesture particularly meaningful is how it acknowledges femininity without objectification. The waist isn't primarily sexual, yet it's distinctly feminine—allowing your touch to celebrate her womanhood while remaining appropriate and respectful. It's appreciation of form that honours rather than reduces.

Phrase to Say

"You have the most beautiful shape." OR This gesture often speaks most eloquently without words—letting appreciative touch communicate directly.

Tips to Make It Work

- **Direction:** Move your hand from the lower rib area down to the hip in one fluid, appreciative motion.
- **Pressure:** Use a touch firm enough to be intentional but light enough to feel appreciative rather than possessive.
- **Context:** Ensure this touch occurs in contexts where physical appreciation feels natural and welcome, not abrupt or disconnected from your existing interaction.

When to Use

This gesture creates connection during embraces, while standing close together, as you pass behind her, or during moments of already established physical proximity. It's particularly meaningful when she's wearing something that accentuates this feature or during moments of expressed appreciation. The key is ensuring the context supports this form of physical acknowledgment.

The Art of Non-Sexual Foreplay

"In true love, the smallest gestures matter the most." —
Hermann Hesse

As we reach seventy gestures in our exploration, this simple truth from Hesse becomes increasingly self-evident. The power of these moments lies not in their grandeur but in their specificity and attention. Each gesture is, at its core, a moment of seeing—truly seeing—the unique person before you. The curve of her waist, the texture of her hair, the space below her ear that responds to gentle kisses—these aren't generic appreciations but highly personal recognitions. In a culture that often defaults to generic expressions of affection, this detailed attention becomes revolutionary. Through these small gestures, you tell her repeatedly: I am paying attention to the particular miracle that is you.

Chapter 71
Resting Your Hand Lightly on Her Thigh During a Quiet Moment

Why It Helps

The gentle weight of a hand resting on her thigh during conversation or shared activity creates a physical anchor point of connection without demanding response. This unobtrusive touch communicates: *I want to maintain physical connection with you even as we engage with other things; my awareness of you continues alongside whatever else we're doing.*

What makes this gesture particularly effective is its balance between intimacy and casualness. The thigh represents more personal territory than hands or arms, yet this placement can feel natural and comfortable rather than intrusive when done with appropriate awareness. It creates sustained connection without requiring either person to shift focus from the primary activity.

Phrase to Say

This gesture typically needs no verbal acknowledgment—it works best as a quiet physical constant beneath whatever else is being discussed or experienced. If anything, perhaps: A gentle squeeze at a relevant moment in conversation. OR "I love these quiet moments together."

Tips to Make It Work

- **Placement:** Rest your hand on the top or outer thigh, avoiding the inner thigh which carries more intimate associations.
- **Pressure:** Keep your touch light but definite—present enough to be felt as intentional connection but not so heavy as to feel restrictive.
- **Stability:** Allow your hand to remain relatively still rather than constantly moving or stroking, creating a steady anchor point rather than active caress.

When to Use

This gesture creates beautiful connection during conversations, while watching films, during car journeys, or any situation where you're sitting alongside each other. It's particularly effective during discussions where emotional support is valuable, creating physical reassurance alongside verbal exchange.

Chapter 72
Guiding Her Into a Slow, Impromptu Dance

Why It Helps

There's something unexpectedly romantic about creating a dance where no formal dance floor exists. When you gently guide her into a slow sway—perhaps in the garden, or beside the car after an evening out, in the middle of a walk in the countryside—you're transforming ordinary space into something momentarily enchanted. This spontaneous movement says: *Our connection can create its own occasion, turning any moment into something worth celebrating.*

The power of this gesture lies in its contrast with everyday practical movement. Most daily motion serves function—walking to get somewhere, reaching to obtain something. Dance exists purely for pleasure and connection, making it a physical declaration that this moment is about nothing except enjoying each other's presence.

Phrase to Say

"Dance with me for a moment." OR "I just need to hold you like this for a minute," as you begin to sway.

Tips to Make It Work

- **Initiation:** Begin with a simple gesture—extending your hand, opening your arms, or placing your hands lightly on her waist in clear invitation.
- **Simplicity:** Keep the movement uncomplicated—this isn't about performance but about shared rhythm and closeness.
- **Adaptability:** Be willing to modify based on available space, accommodating furniture or surroundings while maintaining the essential connected movement.

When to Use

This gesture creates magical moments in otherwise ordinary settings—while out for a walk, after an activity, in the middle of a shop, or even in a car park after a nice but not particularly special outing. It's particularly effective as a pattern interrupt during routine activities, elevating an unremarkable moment into something memorable.

Chapter 73
Kissing the Top of Her Head While Holding Her Close

Why It Helps

There's something profoundly protective about the kiss placed on the crown of her head during an embrace. This gesture combines physical shelter—your body typically enveloping hers from a slight height advantage—with tender affection expressed at her highest point. This protective touch communicates: *I want to shelter you completely while honouring you with affection.*

What makes this gesture particularly meaningful is how it simultaneously acknowledges physical differences while creating emotional equality. The height difference that often allows this gesture isn't about dominance but about complementary fit—two different forms creating perfect connection through their unique shapes.

Phrase to Say

This gesture typically needs no words—the physical connection speaks eloquently on its own. If anything, perhaps: A contented sigh or hum. OR A simple "I've got you" or "I love you" whispered against her hair.

Tips to Make It Work

- **Embrace:** Create a full-body connection rather than just leaning down for the kiss—let your arms encircle her as your lips touch her head.
- **Duration:** Allow your lips to linger for a moment rather than giving a perfunctory peck—this transforms the gesture from casual to meaningful.
- **Pressure:** Keep the kiss gentle but definite—firm enough to be felt through her hair but not pressing heavily downward.

When to Use

This gesture creates beautiful connection during greetings and farewells, moments of comfort or protection, or simply as a spontaneous expression of affection while passing. It's particularly powerful during times of vulnerability or after she's shared something difficult, offering physical reassurance alongside wordless affection.

NOTE: If you're the same height or she is taller, do this when she's sitting on the couch or in a chair, or sitting on the ground/ grass!

Chapter 74
Brushing Your Fingers Over the Inside of Her Wrist

Why It Helps

The inside of the wrist represents one of the body's most vulnerable and sensitive areas—skin is thin, veins are visible, and pulse is palpable. When you deliberately brush your fingers across this delicate region, you're acknowledging this vulnerability with appropriate gentleness. This considered touch says: *I'm aware of your most delicate aspects and approach them with equal parts appreciation and care.*

What makes this gesture particularly effective is its combination of biological significance and subtle execution. The wrist contains a visible pulse point—a literal window to her life force—yet the touch remains light and non-intrusive. It's intimate without being overwhelming, personal without being invasive.

Phrase to Say

"Your skin is so soft here." OR This gesture often works best without words, letting the sensation speak for itself.

Tips to Make It Work

- **Lightness:** Use the gentlest possible touch—just enough pressure to be felt without pressing into the pulse point.
- **Direction:** Move your fingertips across the inner wrist rather than grasping or encircling it, creating sensation without restriction. Light figures of eight often seem to work too.
- **Focus:** Bring full attention to this small point of connection rather than touching absentmindedly while focused elsewhere.

When to Use

This gesture creates meaningful connection during hand-holding, while helping with jewellery or watches, or during moments of already established physical proximity. It's particularly effective during quiet conversations or transitional moments, creating a small but significant point of intimate contact that acknowledges vulnerability without exploiting it.

Chapter 75
Pulling Her Into Your Lap During Relaxed Conversation

Why It Helps

Creating space for her on your lap during relaxed time together establishes a physically close position that combines support, containment, and face-to-face connection. This inviting gesture says: *I want to hold you close while we connect, creating our own intimate space within this environment.*

The effectiveness of this gesture comes from its combination of casual intimacy with focused attention. Unlike side-by-side seating that directs both people outward, this position creates an inward-facing arrangement that prioritises your connection with each other over everything else in the room. It transforms ordinary conversation into something distinctly private and close.

Phrase to Say

"Come here for a minute," with a pat on your lap. OR "I need you a bit closer for this conversation," offered with a warm smile.

Tips to Make It Work

- **Comfort:** Ensure your position provides actual support—a stable base with good back support rather than a precarious perch.
- **Positioning:** Find an arrangement that allows comfortable face-to-face interaction without awkward twisting or straining if you're having a conversation. Or provide a pillow / sweater if it's just for connecting.
- **Duration:** Be attentive to physical comfort over time—what feels connecting initially can become uncomfortable if maintained too long without adjustment.

When to Use

This gesture creates lovely connection during relaxed time at home, while sharing stories or memories, during light-hearted conversations, or when transitioning between activities. It's particularly effective when you want to create a sense of special closeness within an otherwise ordinary interaction, elevating casual conversation into intimate exchange.

Chapter 76
Letting Your Hand Linger on Hers Longer Than Expected

Why It Helps

There's a world of difference between cursory or hasty touch and contact that deliberately extends beyond conventional duration. When you allow your hand to rest on hers for several beats longer than social norms dictate, you're creating a moment that transitions from casual to meaningful through nothing but time. This lingering connection says: *This isn't merely functional contact—I'm choosing to extend this moment of touch because connecting with you matters to me.*

The power lies not in the hand touch itself, which could be entirely ordinary, but in the conscious extension of duration. By allowing the contact to continue past the point where it would typically end, you transform utilitarian touch into emotional connection through nothing but your willingness to remain present in the contact.

Phrase to Say

This gesture typically needs no verbal acknowledgment—its meaning comes specifically from extending beyond words into pure presence. If anything, perhaps: A meaningful glance that coincides with the extended touch. OR A slight squeeze before finally releasing.

Tips to Make It Work

- **Awareness:** Be fully conscious of the duration—this isn't about forgetting to remove your hand but deliberately choosing to extend contact.
- **Pressure:** Maintain gentle but definite contact throughout—neither gripping tightly nor becoming so light the touch becomes ambiguous.
- **Attention:** Keep your focus on the connection rather than continuing conversation or activity as though the touch weren't happening—this awareness is what transforms duration into meaning.

When to Use

This gesture creates beautiful connection during otherwise ordinary exchanges—passing items, momentary hand touches during conversation, or brief contacts while moving through shared space. It's particularly effective during transitions or partings, creating an extended moment of connection before physical separation.

BONUS: As you part, keep the connection all the way down to the fingertips, as if you don't want to let go, but know it's coming.

Chapter 77
Placing a Kiss on Her Closed Eyelids

Why It Helps

Few areas of the body are as vulnerable or as expressive as the eyes. When she closes her eyes to receive your kiss on her eyelids, she's engaging in a profound act of trust—literally suspending her primary means of navigating the world. This extraordinarily gentle gesture says: *I honour the trust you place in me and respond with the most delicate care possible.*

What makes this gesture particularly meaningful is its rarity and deliberateness. Unlike casual touches or even lips-to-lips kissing, this specific form of affection requires both clear intention and perfect gentleness. It acknowledges one of her most physically vulnerable areas with appropriate reverence.

Phrase to Say

"Close your eyes for a moment." OR This gesture often needs no words at all—the extraordinary gentleness speaks for itself.

Tips to Make It Work

- **Approach:** State your intention clearly, either verbally or through slow, deliberate movement that allows her to anticipate and welcome the gesture.
- **Pressure:** Use the lightest possible contact—barely more than your breath against her closed lids.
- **Brevity:** Keep the moment brief—the power comes from the extraordinary gentleness and significance, not from extended duration.

When to Use

This gesture creates profound connection during quiet, intimate moments—while lying close together, during meaningful conversations about feelings, or during particularly tender exchanges. It's especially powerful as an expression of deep care during vulnerable moments or as part of comforting her during difficult emotions.

Chapter 78
Resting Your Hand Lightly Over Her Heart and Feeling Its Rhythm

Why It Helps

There's something intimately connecting about placing your hand gently over someone's heart and feeling its steady rhythm beneath your palm. This mindful touch creates awareness of her most essential life process—the constant, reliable beating that represents her very existence. This reverent gesture says: *I am aware of and grateful for the miracle of your living presence in this world.*

It gives meaning to the phrase "heartfelt".

What distinguishes this gesture is its focus on internal rather than external qualities. Unlike touches that appreciate visible features, this connection acknowledges something typically unseen but absolutely fundamental—the rhythmic pulse that began before her birth and continues every moment without conscious effort.

Phrase to Say

"I love feeling your heartbeat." OR "The most beautiful rhythm in the world."

Tips to Make It Work

- **Placement:** Rest your hand on the left side of her chest, over the heart area but not directly on the breast—maintaining the focus on life essence rather than physical intimacy.
- **Pressure:** Use very light pressure—just enough to feel the subtle rhythm without creating any sense of weight or restriction.
- **Presence:** Bring your full attention to the sensation, perhaps closing your eyes briefly to focus entirely on this connection to her life force.

When to Use

This gesture creates profound connection during quiet moments of closeness—while holding each other, during peaceful rest together, after meaningful conversations, or during moments of expressed gratitude for each other. It's particularly powerful during transitions in your relationship —anniversaries, after resolving conflicts, or when feeling especially appreciative of her presence in your life.

BONUS: Being a sensory person, I love resting my ear over her heart and hearing the heartbeat. Even big guys like me enjoy that peaceful calming rhythm.

Chapter 79
Lightly Tracing the Outline of Her Collarbone with Your Fingertips

Why It Helps

The collarbone represents one of the body's most visually distinctive structures—a graceful architectural element that frames the transition from neck to shoulder. When you delicately trace this contour with your fingertips, you're acknowledging the beautiful physical structure that makes her unique. This appreciative exploration says: *I notice and admire even the fundamental framework that makes you who you are.*

What makes this gesture particularly effective is its combination of structural acknowledgment with gentle sensation. You're simultaneously appreciating her form and creating pleasant physical awareness along a ridge that contains numerous nerve endings. It's admiration that can be both seen in your focus and felt in her body.

Phrase to Say

"You have such beautiful lines." OR This gesture often works best without words, letting your focused attention and touch speak for themselves.

Tips to Make It Work

- **Lightness:** Use the barest whisper of contact—just enough pressure for your fingertip to maintain connection without pressing into the bone.
- **Direction:** Follow the natural curve from the base of her neck outward toward the shoulder, treating the contour as a deliberate path.
- **Pace:** Move slowly enough that the gesture feels like appreciation rather than casual contact—the intentional pace transforms touch into admiration.

When to Use

This gesture creates beautiful connection during intimate conversations, quiet moments together, or times of expressed appreciation. It's particularly effective when she's wearing clothing that reveals this area, acknowledging the beauty of what's visible without drawing explicit attention to exposure.

Chapter 80
Pulling Her in Close During a Deep, Quiet Conversation

Why It Helps

There's something profoundly affirming about being physically drawn closer during moments of emotional vulnerability or intellectual depth. When you gently pull her nearer as conversation moves into meaningful territory, you're creating physical closeness that mirrors and supports emotional openness. This synchronised gesture says: *As we move deeper in words, I want us closer in presence—connection on all levels simultaneously.*

The power of this gesture lies in its responsive timing. By initiating closer physical proximity specifically when conversation deepens, you're creating tangible reassurance that vulnerability and closeness belong together—that opening emotionally or intellectually doesn't create distance but rather deserves greater connection.

Phrase to Say

"Come a little closer—I want to really hear this." OR Simply extend your arm in clear invitation as the conversation shifts to deeper territory.

Tips to Make It Work

- **Gentleness:** Make the drawing-in motion an invitation rather than a demand—a suggestion of closeness that she can lean into rather than a pull she must respond to.
- **Positioning:** Create an arrangement that allows continued comfortable eye contact during the conversation—physical closeness should enhance rather than complicate verbal connection.
- **Attention:** Maintain complete focus on what she's saying as you bring her physically closer—this gesture is about supporting her expression, not distracting from it.

When to Use

This gesture creates stronger connection during important discussions, vulnerable sharing, moments of reminiscence, or any conversation that moves beyond surface pleasantries. It's particularly meaningful when she's sharing something difficult or important, creating physical reassurance precisely when emotional exposure might otherwise create feelings of vulnerability.

Nolan Collins

"It's not what you look at that matters, it's what you see."
— Henry David Thoreau

As we continue exploring these gestures, Thoreau's distinction between looking and seeing becomes increasingly relevant. The gestures in this section—feeling her heartbeat, tracing her collarbone, drawing her close during vulnerability—require more than mechanical observation. They demand a quality of perception that penetrates beyond the obvious. To truly see someone is to perceive the miracle of their heartbeat, the elegant architecture of their bone structure, the courage in their vulnerable words. These gestures are physical expressions of that deeper seeing, tangible evidence that you're paying a quality of attention that most people never receive. When practised consistently, they create a relationship where both people feel not merely observed but truly perceived in their full humanity.

Chapter 81
Running Your Thumb Over Her Lips with a Tender Smile

Why It Helps

The lips represent one of our most expressive and sensitive features—used for communication, emotion, and connection. When you gently run your thumb across this responsive area while offering a warm smile, you're creating a moment of focused appreciation for her expressive essence. This intimate gesture says: *I'm drawn to the part of you that speaks, smiles, and connects—the gateway to your thoughts and feelings*.

What makes this gesture particularly meaningful is its directed attention. Unlike a kiss, which engages both people equally, this touch allows you to observe her response while creating the sensation—to witness the effect of your appreciation in real time. It combines giving pleasure with appreciative observation in a uniquely connected moment.

Phrase to Say

"You have the most expressive lips." or "Your lips are like marshsmallows. A little chocolate and it's like kissing smores!" OR This gesture often communicates most powerfully through your expression rather than words—a warm smile or softened look says everything necessary.

Tips to Make It Work

- **Approach:** Move slowly and with clear intention, allowing her to anticipate and welcome the contact rather than being surprised by it.
- **Pressure:** Use the lightest possible touch—just enough to create distinct sensation without pressing or manipulating the shape of her lips.
- **Focus:** Maintain eye contact during this gesture unless she closes her eyes in response, creating dual connection through both touch and sight.

When to Use

This gesture creates beautiful connection during intimate conversations, quiet moments of appreciation, or as a prelude to kissing without immediately initiating it. It's particularly effective during pauses in conversation or moments of natural silence, creating physical connection that acknowledges the importance of her expression.

Chapter 82
Placing a Kiss on Her Shoulder While Embracing Her

Why It Helps

The shoulder carries both literal and metaphorical significance—it bears weight, supports burdens, and forms part of our physical framework. When you place a deliberate kiss on this strong yet vulnerable area during an embrace, you're acknowledging both her strength and her need for tenderness. This thoughtful gesture says: *I appreciate both your capacity to carry life's weight and your need for care in doing so.*

What distinguishes this from other forms of embrace-kissing is its location—neither the expected head/face region nor more intimate areas, but this uniquely structural part that represents capability and support. It acknowledges her physical strength while offering affection that honours rather than diminishes that power.

Phrase to Say

This gesture typically needs no verbal accompaniment—the sensation itself communicates everything necessary. If anything, perhaps: A contented sigh against her skin. OR "You carry so much—I notice that."

Tips to Make It Work

- **Placement:** Kiss the curve where neck meets shoulder or the rounded outer edge—areas that are both accessible and sensitive. Work your way up the neck to the ear for a more intimate experience, moving her hair out of the way at the same time.
- **Pressure:** Keep the kiss definite but gentle—firm enough to be distinctly felt through clothing but not so intense as to seem demanding.
- **Context:** Incorporate this naturally within an embrace rather than creating a separate, ceremonial gesture— let it feel like an organic expression of appreciation.

When to Use

This gesture creates meaningful connection during embraces of greeting or farewell, moments of comfort or congratulation, or simply as an enhancement to an ordinary hug. It's particularly effective when she's been carrying significant responsibilities or challenges, acknowledging her strength while offering tenderness exactly where she bears weight.

Chapter 83

Resting Your Hand at the Nape of Her Neck During a Hug

Why It Helps

The nape of the neck represents a uniquely vulnerable yet sturdy region—exposed, sensitive, yet supporting the weight of the head. When you rest your hand gently on this area during an embrace, you're creating a point of secure connection in a place rarely touched in ordinary interaction. This protective gesture says: *I'm offering support and connection at one of your most exposed yet essential points.*

The effectiveness of this gesture comes from the particular sensitivity of this region combined with its structural significance. The nape contains numerous nerve endings while also housing the top of the spine—our literal support column. Your touch simultaneously provides pleasure through sensation and symbolic support through location.

Phrase to Say

This gesture typically needs no verbal enhancement—the physical connection speaks eloquently on its own. If anything, perhaps: A simple "I've got you" or "I'm here" spoken softly near her ear.

Tips to Make It Work

- **Placement:** Rest your open palm against the nape with fingers either extending slightly up into hairline or curving gently around the side of the neck.
- **Pressure:** Use gentle but definite contact—enough pressure to create security without any sense of control or restriction.
- **Warmth:** Ensure your hand is warm before placement, as cold hands against this sensitive area can create discomfort rather than connection.

When to Use

This gesture creates beautiful connection during embraces of any kind—greetings, farewells, comfort, or celebration. It's particularly powerful during moments of vulnerability or uncertainty, offering literal and figurative support to her head and thoughts. The simple addition of this hand placement transforms an ordinary hug into something noticeably more supportive and connected.

Chapter 84
Gently Holding Her Foot While Massaging It

Why It Helps

The feet bear our literal weight through life yet receive remarkably little care or appreciation. When you take time to hold her foot carefully while providing gentle massage, you're acknowledging this fundamental but overlooked area with genuine care. This nurturing gesture says: *I see and want to care for even the parts of you that support you without recognition—nothing about you is beneath my attention.*

What makes this gesture particularly meaningful is its element of service without expectation. Foot massage requires giving without immediate reciprocation, creating care that flows in one direction without demand. It's a physical expression of generosity that honours the often unacknowledged foundation of her physical experience.

Phrase to Say

"Let me help you relax a bit." OR "You're on your feet so much —they deserve some attention too."

Tips to Make It Work

- **Position:** Create a comfortable arrangement where her foot is supported, either on your lap or on a cushion, allowing full relaxation.
- **Technique:** Begin with gentle holding and warm-up strokes before addressing specific pressure points— connection before deeper work.
- **Attention:** Focus completely on this task rather than treating it as an absent-minded activity while doing something else. Intention can be felt!

When to Use

This gesture creates wonderful connection after she's been on her feet for extended periods, following a long workday, during relaxation time in the evening, or as part of unwinding before sleep. It's particularly appreciated when offered without prompting, showing your awareness of her comfort needs before she has to express them.

BONUS: This goes for any massage. Listen to her. If she says you're pressing too hard, ease up. Don't take it personally. Don't stop. The trick is to apply gentle pressure. Start with simple circles and gradually increase the pressure. If she winces or pulls away, ease up a bit. Massage in this context is not about how hard or deep you can go, it's about the experience, intention and connection. Trust me on this, I'm also a qualified massage therapist!

Chapter 85
Wrapping Your Fingers Around Hers and Gently Squeezing

Why It Helps

Hand-holding itself is a common connection, but the deliberate wrapping of your fingers around hers with a meaningful squeeze creates a specific moment of communicative touch. This intentional pressure says: *I'm thinking about you right now, with particular focus, even as we continue whatever else we're doing*.

What distinguishes this from ordinary hand-holding is its deliberateness and momentary intensity. Rather than sustained, passive connection, this gesture creates a distinct pulse of communication—a non-verbal "I'm here" or "I'm with you" that punctuates your ongoing physical link with a moment of heightened attention.

Phrase to Say

This gesture typically speaks most eloquently without words —the pressure itself communicates everything necessary. If anything, perhaps: Meeting her eyes briefly as you squeeze, letting your expression convey the meaning.

Tips to Make It Work

- **Timing:** Choose moments where the squeeze carries contextual meaning—during challenging conversations, when something meaningful is said, or at moments of transition.
- **Pressure:** Find that perfect middle ground—firm enough to be clearly intentional but gentle enough to feel like connection rather than control. Don't cut off the blood supply to her fingers!
- **Duration:** Make the squeeze distinct but brief—a communicative pulse rather than a sustained grip—before returning to normal holding pressure.

When to Use

This gesture creates meaningful connection during hand-holding of any kind—while walking, sitting together, or in public settings. It's particularly powerful during conversations where words feel insufficient, during shared experiences (both challenging and joyful), or as silent support when she's facing something difficult. Think of it as punctuation in your physical language—creating emphasis within your ongoing connection.

Chapter 86
Laying Your Hand Over Hers and Intertwining Your Fingers

Why It Helps

The deliberate placement of your hand over hers, followed by the gentle intertwining of fingers, creates a particular form of hand connection that feels both protective and equal. Unlike side-by-side hand-holding, this overlapping arrangement says: *I want to both shelter and connect with you simultaneously—offering both cover and integration.*

What makes this gesture uniquely effective is its layered symbolism. The initial covering offers protection and security, while the subsequent intertwining represents equal partnership and mutual engagement. It transforms a potentially hierarchical gesture into one of balanced connection through the simple addition of finger integration.

Phrase to Say

This gesture typically needs no verbal enhancement—the physical connection speaks for itself. If anything, perhaps: A simple "There" as your fingers slide between hers. OR "I love how our hands fit together."

Tips to Make It Work

- **Approach:** Begin by placing your hand gently over the back of hers, creating the covering aspect before transitioning to intertwined fingers.
- **Adaptation:** Be responsive to her hand positioning, allowing mutual adjustment rather than forcing your fingers into predetermined places.
- **Pressure:** Maintain light but definite contact throughout—present enough to feel connected but not restricting her ability to adjust or withdraw if desired.

When to Use

This gesture creates beautiful connection during conversations, while offering support, during moments of shared experience, or simply as a way of establishing physical link while engaged in other activities. It's particularly effective during moments that blend vulnerability with partnership—situations where both protection and equality are meaningful elements of your connection.

Chapter 87
Slowly Caressing the Side of Her Neck with Your Palm

Why It Helps

The side of the neck represents one of the body's most vulnerable yet sensitive regions—containing vital pathways while being relatively unprotected by bone or muscle. When you gently caress this area with your palm, you're acknowledging this vulnerability with appropriate care. This attentive touch says: *I'm aware of your most exposed areas and approach them with protective appreciation rather than exploitation.*

What makes this gesture particularly meaningful is the contrast between the area's vulnerability and your gentle approach. Rather than using this exposure as opportunity for control, you're offering careful attention that honours both the sensitivity and the trust implied in allowing contact here.

Phrase to Say

"Your skin is so soft here." OR This gesture often works best without words, letting the sensation speak for itself.

Tips to Make It Work

- **Direction:** Move your palm from just below the ear downward toward the collarbone in a fluid, unhurried motion.
- **Pressure:** Use very light contact—just enough to create pleasant sensation without any sense of pressure against the throat area.
- **Attention:** Bring complete focus to this gesture rather than touching absentmindedly—the quality of your attention transforms it from casual contact to meaningful connection.
- **Position:** If you have large hands, and she has a small neck, tilt her head to the side to expose a longer surface and place your hand against her neck, cradling her neck and head instead of caressing.

When to Use

This gesture creates connection during quiet moments of closeness, intimate conversations, or transitions between activities. It's particularly effective as a brief but meaningful touch while passing behind her chair, during an embrace, or as part of a greeting that acknowledges your appreciation for her presence.

Chapter 88
Leaning In to Softly Kiss Her Forehead in a Lingering Way

Why It Helps

The forehead kiss occupies unique territory in physical affection—neither romantic in the way of lip kisses nor casual like cheek kisses. When you lean in to place a deliberate, lingering kiss on her forehead, you're engaging in a distinctly protective form of affection. This nurturing gesture says: *I care for you in a way that transcends passion alone—I want to shelter and cherish you completely*.

What distinguishes this gesture is its combination of height advantage and deliberate gentleness. You're typically in a physically protective position while offering the most tender form of contact—creating simultaneously the sense of being both protected and profoundly valued.

Phrase to Say

This gesture typically needs no verbal accompaniment—the lingering contact speaks eloquently on its own. If anything, perhaps: A soft exhale or hum of appreciation against her skin. OR A simple "Sleep well" or "Be safe" if it's a parting gesture.

Tips to Make It Work

- **Approach:** Move with unhurried deliberateness, allowing her to anticipate and welcome the gesture rather than being surprised by it.
- **Duration:** Let your lips remain in contact for a moment longer than a perfunctory kiss—long enough to convey intention without becoming uncomfortable.
- **Completion:** As you withdraw, maintain eye contact briefly, acknowledging the moment of connection rather than immediately moving to another activity.

When to Use

This gesture creates powerful connection during greetings and farewells, moments of comfort or reassurance, or as recognition of her vulnerability. It's particularly meaningful during transitions—before she leaves for a journey, after she's shared something difficult, before sleep, or when departing for separate activities—creating a protective blessing that lingers beyond your physical presence.

Chapter 89
Letting Your Hand Settle Just Above Her Knee While Sitting Close

Why It Helps

The area just above the knee occupies an interesting middle territory—neither as casual as touching a hand nor as intimate as the upper thigh. When you rest your hand in this region while sitting together, you're establishing physical connection that is both definite and respectful. This considerate touch says: *I want to maintain physical connection with you in a way that's present but not presumptuous.*

The effectiveness of this gesture comes from its clear intentionality combined with boundary respect. Unlike an arm around shoulders (which can feel casual) or hand higher on the thigh (which carries more intimate implications), this placement creates deliberate connection while acknowledging appropriate limits.

Phrase to Say

This gesture typically needs no verbal acknowledgment—it works best as a quiet physical complement to whatever conversation or activity is already happening. If anything, perhaps: A gentle squeeze at a relevant moment in conversation.

Tips to Make It Work

- **Placement:** Position your hand on the lower thigh just above the knee, typically on the outer side rather than inner thigh.
- **Pressure:** Keep your touch light but present—definite enough to be felt as intentional connection but not so heavy as to feel restrictive.
- **Stillness:** Allow your hand to rest quietly rather than actively stroking or squeezing constantly, creating steady presence rather than demanding attention.

When to Use

This gesture creates lovely connection during conversations, while watching films, during car journeys, or any situation where you're sitting alongside each other. It's particularly effective in public or social settings where more intimate contact might feel inappropriate, creating a clear point of connection that respects the context of your surroundings.

Chapter 90
Grazing Your Knuckles Along Her Arm in a Slow, Comforting Motion

Why It Helps

There's something distinctly comforting about the sensation of knuckles—their rounded firmness creating a different quality of touch than fingertips or palms. When you slowly graze your knuckles along her arm from shoulder to wrist, you're providing a unique tactile experience that is simultaneously substantial and gentle. This nurturing touch says: *I want to provide both grounding and pleasant sensation— security and enjoyment in a single gesture.*

What makes this particularly effective is how it combines firmness with gentleness. Unlike light fingertip touches that can sometimes feel ticklish or fleeting, knuckles provide more definite contact while still remaining completely non-threatening. It's a touch that feels stable and reliable while remaining entirely gentle.

Phrase to Say

This gesture typically needs no verbal enhancement—it works best as a quiet physical language of comfort. If anything, perhaps: "Just relax" as you begin the motion. OR "Your skin is so soft," spoken quietly during the touch.

Tips to Make It Work

- **Direction:** Move from shoulder downward toward hand in a smooth, continuous motion rather than short back-and-forth strokes.
- **Speed:** Keep the movement deliberately slow—this is about sustained comfort rather than quick stimulation.
- **Pressure:** Find that perfect middle ground where your knuckles maintain contact without pressing deeply—present but not heavy.

When to Use

This gesture creates wonderful connection during quiet moments together, while she's resting against you, during conversations about difficult topics, or as part of helping her relax after stress. It's particularly effective when she seems tense or overwhelmed, offering a grounding physical connection that helps regulate emotional states through steady, predictable touch.

The Art of Non-Sexual Foreplay

"The greatest compliment that was ever paid me was when one asked me what I thought, and attended to my answer." — Henry David Thoreau

As we approach the conclusion of our exploration, this insight from Thoreau illuminates the deeper principle behind all these gestures. While we've focused on physical expressions of attention, the essence of each action is the quality of noticing that precedes it. To trace her collarbone, you must first notice its elegant line. To kiss her forehead lingeringly, you must first recognise her need for gentle affection. To squeeze her hand meaningfully, you must first be attuned to the moment when such connection matters most. Each gesture in this collection is, at its heart, a physical manifestation of the greatest gift we can offer another human: our complete, undivided, appreciative attention.

Chapter 91
Pulling Her In So She Can Rest Her Head on Your Chest

Why It Helps

The human chest—particularly for men—provides a unique combination of softness and structural stability, creating an ideal resting place for her head. When you gently guide her to this position, you're offering both literal and metaphorical support. This sheltering gesture says: *Rest against my strength; let me hold you while you momentarily release the need to hold yourself up.*

What makes this particularly meaningful is the physical reality of your heartbeat beneath her ear. This sound—the most fundamental rhythm of your existence—becomes her direct experience, creating an intimacy that transcends the merely physical. She's not just near you but essentially within you, experiencing your life force as a tactile sensation.

Phrase to Say

"Come here for a moment," as you create space for her. OR "Just rest here for a bit," as your hand guides her head gently to your chest.

Tips to Make It Work

- **Positioning:** Create a comfortable angle that allows her head to rest naturally without strain on her neck —slightly reclined often works best.
- **Stability:** Maintain steady breathing and a stable position that allows her to fully relax against you without constant adjustment.
- **Duration:** Allow this connection to last as long as it feels comfortable for both of you—this isn't a momentary gesture but a sustained position of shared peace.

When to Use

This gesture creates a heartfelt connection after emotional discussions, during quiet evenings together, when she seems weary or overwhelmed, or simply as a way of building intimacy during ordinary moments. It's particularly powerful during times of stress or uncertainty, providing literal stability that translates to emotional security.

Chapter 92
Stroking Her Hairline as She Falls Asleep Beside You

Why It Helps

The transition from wakefulness to sleep represents one of our most vulnerable daily surrenders. When you gently stroke her hairline as she drifts toward unconsciousness, you're creating a safe container for this vulnerability. This protective gesture says: *I'll attend to you even as you release conscious control; your security remains my priority as you transition to your most defenceless state.*

What distinguishes this touch is its perfect balance of presence and non-intrusion. The hairline provides stimulation subtle enough not to prevent sleep while definite enough to register as intentional care. It creates the reassuring awareness of your attention without demanding her continued consciousness to receive it.

Phrase to Say

"Sleep well, beautiful." OR This gesture often works best with no words at all—perhaps just the softest humming or rhythmic breathing that helps guide her toward rest.

Tips to Make It Work

- **Lightness:** Use the gentlest possible touch—just enough to create pleasant sensation without being stimulating enough to prevent sleep.
- **Rhythm:** Maintain a slow, predictable pattern that becomes almost hypnotic in its consistency, helping guide her nervous system toward relaxation.
- **Patience:** Continue the gesture well past the point where you think she might be asleep—the transition occurs gradually, and your touch remains comforting even in early sleep stages.

When to Use

This gesture creates beautiful connection during bedtime or nap time, particularly when she's had a challenging day, is having trouble quieting her mind, or has expressed feeling unsettled. It's especially powerful as part of a consistent sleep ritual, creating a reliable transition that her body and mind come to associate with security and rest.

Chapter 93
Gently Brushing Your Fingers Across Her Jawline and Pausing at Her Chin

Why It Helps

The jawline represents one of the face's most distinctive structural elements—a feature that literally frames her expression and defines her profile. When you trace this contour with deliberate appreciation, pausing momentarily at the chin, you're acknowledging her unique facial architecture. This attentive gesture says: *I see and value the very framework of your facial identity—the structure that makes you distinctively you.*

What makes this particularly meaningful is its focus on a feature that's fundamental rather than decorative. Unlike appreciating makeup or hairstyle, this acknowledges something intrinsic to her physical form—an appreciation that can't be attributed to artificial enhancement but only to her essential self.

Phrase to Say

"You have such a beautiful profile." OR This gesture often communicates most effectively without words—your focused attention speaks volumes by itself.

Tips to Make It Work

- **Approach:** Begin at the ear area and follow the natural line toward her chin with unhurried appreciation.
- **Touch:** Use the backs of your fingers or knuckles for the tracing motion, then perhaps transition to a gentle thumb and forefinger to briefly hold her chin at the conclusion.
- **Gaze:** Maintain gentle eye contact during this gesture if her position allows, creating dual connection through both touch and sight.

When to Use

This gesture creates lovely connection during quiet moments of appreciation, intimate conversations, or transitional times between activities. It's particularly effective when natural light highlights her profile, drawing your genuine appreciation to this defining feature and translating that recognition into physical acknowledgment.

Chapter 94
Running Your Fingers Down the Length of Her Spine in a Light Touch

Why It Helps

The spine represents our literal central support—the structural column that enables both stability and movement. When you trace this fundamental line from neck to lower back, you're acknowledging her core physical architecture with appreciation. This mindful gesture says: *I recognise and honour the essential framework that supports everything else about you.*

What distinguishes this touch is its connection to her most central physical structure. Unlike more superficial caresses, this traces the very column of her skeletal system—the line from which all other physical movement becomes possible. It's a touch that honours function and form simultaneously.

Phrase to Say

"Your back is so beautiful." OR This gesture often works most powerfully without words—the deliberate tracing speaks eloquently on its own.

Tips to Make It Work

- **Direction:** Move from the nape of the neck downward in one fluid, continuous motion rather than separate touches.
- **Pressure:** Use very light contact—just enough to be distinctly felt without pressing into the vertebrae themselves.
- **Pace:** Move slowly enough that the gesture feels like appreciation rather than casual contact—the intentional pace transforms touch into admiration.

When to Use

This gesture creates beautiful connection when she's facing away from you, while embracing from behind, during massage transitions, or as a brief appreciative touch while passing. It's particularly effective when she's wearing clothing that exposes or emphasises the back, acknowledging this often-overlooked aspect of her physical presence.

Chapter 95
Guiding Her Face Toward Yours with a Light Touch to Her Cheek

Why It Helps

There's something about the gentle guidance of her face toward yours. When you place light fingers against her cheek to create this reorientation, you're requesting visual connection in the most respectful way possible. This inviting gesture says: *I want to see you more directly; I'm drawn to your face and expressions and invite you to share them with me.*

The power of this gesture lies in its perfect balance between direction and respect. You're expressing a clear desire for greater connection while using the lightest possible touch to suggest rather than demand this shift. It acknowledges both your wish for closer engagement and her freedom to respond as she chooses.

Phrase to Say

"I want to see your face." OR This gesture often communicates most effectively through your expression as her eyes meet yours—a warm smile or softened gaze that shows appreciation for the connection.

204

Tips to Make It Work

- **Lightness:** Use minimal pressure against her cheek—just enough to suggest the direction rather than physically moving her face.
- **Patience:** Allow her to complete the movement at her own pace rather than rushing the reorientation.
- **Acknowledgment:** Once your eyes meet, show appreciation through your expression, completing the purpose of the gesture with appropriate recognition.

When to Use

This gesture creates meaningful connection during conversations where she's looking away, moments when you want to transition from casual interaction to more focused engagement, or times when you want to express particular appreciation for her facial expressions. It's especially effective as a gentle intervention when she seems lost in thought, creating an invitation back to shared presence.

Chapter 96
Pressing Your Lips Softly to the Inside of Her Wrist

Why It Helps

The inside of the wrist contains one of the body's most vulnerable and sensitive areas—where skin is thin, veins are visible, and pulse is tangible. When you bring your lips to this delicate region with deliberate gentleness, you're acknowledging this vulnerability with appropriate reverence. This intimate gesture says: *I approach your most delicate aspects with equal measures of desire and respect*.

What makes this particularly meaningful is its connection to her literal life force. The pulse point you kiss contains the visible rhythm of her existence—a direct connection to her heart's work. This creates a moment of profound intimacy that honours her most essential functioning with the gentlest possible acknowledgment.

Phrase to Say

This gesture typically needs no verbal enhancement—the sensation itself communicates everything necessary. If anything, perhaps: A soft "Mmm" of appreciation against her skin. OR "I can feel your pulse" spoken quietly with wonder.

Tips to Make It Work

- **Approach:** Lift her hand gently, turning the wrist upward with clear but unhurried intention.
- **Contact:** Keep the kiss feather-light—just enough pressure to be distinctly felt without pressing against the pulse point.
- **Duration:** Allow your lips to linger just long enough to acknowledge the significance without creating discomfort about the vulnerability of the area.

When to Use

This gesture creates beautiful connection during quiet moments together, as a greeting or farewell with particular meaning, or during transitions between activities. It's especially powerful as a wordless expression of appreciation —the kiss that acknowledges her essence rather than just her appearance or actions.

Chapter 97
Placing a Lingering Hand on Her Hip as You Walk Past

Why It Helps

The brief but deliberate placement of your hand on her hip as you move through shared space creates a moment of physical acknowledgment within ordinary movement. This passing touch says: *Even in transition, I'm aware of and drawn to you— my attention remains with you despite my changing location.*

What distinguishes this from casual contact is its intentional quality and slight extension of duration. Rather than an incidental brush, this deliberate pause in your movement creates a moment of connection that acknowledges her presence as significant enough to interrupt your trajectory, if only briefly.

Phrase to Say

This gesture typically speaks most eloquently without words —the brief pause in movement communicates everything necessary. If anything, perhaps: A soft "Hey you" as you pass. OR A simple smile that accompanies the touch, acknowledging the moment of connection.

Tips to Make It Work

- **Placement:** Rest your hand lightly on the side of her hip or waist—a neutral zone that feels connecting without being overly intimate.
- **Pressure:** Use gentle but definite contact—firm enough to be clearly intentional but light enough to feel like appreciation rather than direction.
- **Duration:** Extend the touch just slightly beyond what would feel casual—long enough to register as deliberate connection but brief enough to maintain the "in passing" quality.

When to Use

This gesture creates lovely connection during everyday movement through shared spaces—passing in the kitchen, moving through a doorway, or navigating around furniture. It's particularly effective during busy periods when extended interaction isn't possible, creating brief but meaningful points of contact that maintain connection amid separate activities.

Chapter 98
Wrapping Her Hands in Yours and Warming Them with Your Breath

Why It Helps

Cold hands create a perfect opportunity for practical care that simultaneously builds intimacy. When you envelop her chilled fingers between your palms and gently warm them with your breath, you're addressing a physical need while creating profound connection. This nurturing gesture says: *I notice your discomfort and am literally sharing my warmth to improve your experience.*

What makes this particularly effective is its combination of multiple intimate elements: the complete enclosure of her hands within yours, the sharing of your breath (one of the most fundamental life exchanges), and the practical improvement in her comfort. It's care that operates on both symbolic and literal levels simultaneously.

Phrase to Say

"Let me warm these up for you." OR "Your hands are freezing —here, let me help with that."

Tips to Make It Work

- **Enclosure:** Fully surround her hands with yours, creating a protective cave of warmth rather than just holding the fingertips.
- **Breath:** Blow gently with warm (not hot) breath, creating consistent warmth without uncomfortable moisture.
- **Attention:** Focus completely on this task rather than treating it as an absent-minded activity—your full attention transforms functional warming into intimate care.

When to Use

This gesture creates beautiful connection during cold weather outings, after she's been outside, when entering a warm space from cold conditions, or anytime you notice her hands feeling chilled. It's particularly appreciated as a spontaneous response to her discomfort rather than waiting for her to request warmth.

Chapter 99
Stroking Her Temple with Your Thumb as You Look Into Her Eyes

Why It Helps

The temple represents a uniquely vulnerable facial area— where skin is thin, the pulse is often visible, and protective bone structure is minimal. When you stroke this delicate region with your thumb while maintaining eye contact, you're creating dual connection at two of her most sensitive points. This intimate gesture says: *I'm present with you completely—attending to both your expressions and your physical comfort simultaneously.*

What makes this particularly powerful is the combination of touch and gaze. The physical contact provides tactile comfort while eye connection creates emotional presence—a holistic form of attention that acknowledges both her body and her consciousness in perfect synchronicity.

Phrase to Say

"I love looking at you like this." OR This gesture often communicates most effectively without words—your expression and touch create complete connection without verbal enhancement.

Tips to Make It Work

- **Position:** Rest your hand along the side of her face with your thumb at her temple and fingers extending back toward her ear or hair.
- **Movement:** Make the thumb motion gentle and rhythmic—small circles or light strokes that create soothing consistency.
- **Gaze:** Maintain soft but definite eye contact, creating the sense of complete attention rather than just physical touch.

When to Use

This gesture creates profound connection during intimate conversations, moments of reassurance, expressions of affection, or times of wordless appreciation. It's particularly effective during transitions—before parting for the day, upon reuniting after separation, or when shifting from ordinary interaction to deeper connection.

BONUS: If she's got a headache, gently rub her temples, above and to the side of her eyes. Gentle circlular motion works well, or simply place your fingers there and feel her pulse intensify into your fingers. Keep a light touch, and offer her some water to help release some tension.

Chapter 100
Creating a Bubble of Intimacy by Touching Foreheads and Sharing Breath

Why It Helps

Few gestures create more immediate intimacy than the gentle meeting of foreheads with shared breath between you. This position establishes a literal shared space—your exhales becoming her inhales in a continuous exchange of life essence. This profound connection says: *We exist in our own world now, sharing the most fundamental elements of existence in perfect proximity.*

What makes this our culminating gesture is its completeness. It combines physical connection, shared sustenance (breath), matching vulnerability (both equally exposed), and perfect symmetry (neither leading nor following). It's perhaps the purest expression of equal, respectful intimacy possible between two people—a complete meeting of separate beings in willing, conscious connection.

Phrase to Say

This gesture typically needs no verbal enhancement—the physical connection speaks with perfect eloquence. If anything, perhaps: The softest whisper of "Just us" or "Here we are." OR Simply an audible, contented exhale that says everything words cannot.

Tips to Make It Work

- **Approach:** Move slowly into position, allowing mutual adjustment to find the most comfortable meeting point.
- **Pressure:** Find that perfect balance where your foreheads connect definitively without either person bearing uncomfortable weight.
- **Breath:** Be conscious of your breathing—keeping it gentle, regular, and fresh, creating pleasant sharing rather than overwhelming proximity. Have a mint if you've just finished eating BBQ, fish or garlic!

When to Use

This gesture creates extraordinary connection during moments of deep emotional significance—expressions of love, reconciliations after conflict, celebrations of relationship milestones, or times when words simply cannot contain what needs to be expressed. It's the physical embodiment of complete presence with another human being—the gesture that acknowledges no distance remains between you.

Nolan Collins

The Art of Seeing

Your fingertips trace paths only you can see —
The architecture of her collarbone,
The delicate hollow beneath her ear,
The curve where neck meets shoulder.
You map her like a country only you explore,
Not with conquest in mind
But with reverence for the landscape.
Your eyes hold questions your lips never form —
How did the universe arrange itself
To place her here, within reach?
What miracle of timing and chance
Created this moment where your breath
Mingles with hers in shared space?
These are mysteries you solve with presence.
Your hands speak languages without grammar —
The dialect of a palm against her back,
The syntax of fingers through her hair,
The eloquence of thumbs tracing temples.
You write poems on her skin that disappear
The moment they're composed,
Yet somehow she remembers every word.
The art lies not in grand gestures
But in the spaces between heartbeats,
In the momentary pauses between breaths,
In the silent agreement that this —
This ordinary Tuesday evening,
This unremarkable moment of existing together —
Is actually everything.

Wrapping It All Up: Your Journey Starts Now

So there you have it—100 ways to create moments of connection that have nothing to do with sex and everything to do with intimacy. Pretty cool, right?

Here's the thing about these gestures that I really want you to take away: they're not some kind of relationship checklist to stress about. You don't need to memorise them or worry about getting them "right." They're more like a toolbox you can dip into whenever you want to create a moment that says, "Hey, I see you. The real you. And I'm actually paying attention."

The magic isn't in the perfect execution of running your fingers through her hair or tracing her collarbone just so. The magic is in the fact that you're fully there when you do it— present, focused, and genuinely interested in the amazing person you're with.

Think about it: when was the last time you felt someone was 100% there with you? Not checking their phone, not mentally making a grocery list, not waiting for their turn to talk—but actually there? Pretty rare, right? That's the real gift you're giving with these gestures.

What I've found in my own relationships is that these small moments of connection aren't just nice extras—they're the glue that holds everything together when life gets messy. That hand squeeze during a stressful family dinner or that knowing smile across a crowded room can say more than a thousand words. They also say "I'm here and I've got you."

You'll forget these sometimes. You'll do them awkwardly other times. There will be days when you're too tired or stressed to think about forehead kisses or active listening. That's just being human. The point isn't perfection—it's coming back to this intention of seeing her, again and again, even when it's difficult. Especially when it's difficult.

Start small. Maybe pick one or two gestures that feel natural to you and weave them into your day. Notice what happens. Notice how it feels—for both of you. Then try something else. Let this become a living, evolving practice rather than another thing to get "right."

Remember, the woman in your life doesn't need you to be perfect. She needs you to be present. Everything else flows from that simple truth.

So here's to all the small moments that build something big. Here's to the art of paying attention. Here's to seeing the extraordinary in ordinary Tuesdays, and to the kind of intimacy that has nothing to prove and everything to give.

Your journey into this art of connection starts now. And trust me—it's worth every step.

Whats next?

Don't forget! Here's how...

If you're like me, you want to do better, but often forget. I started putting reminders in my phone to do "something" but invariably forgot when I couldnt think of something specific.

For that reason I now offer a weekly "reminder" email for men that goes out with a suggestion of something you can do. Every. Single. Week.

That's a lot of reminders of different things you can do. Some are mild, some are a bit more spicy (especially on Fridays!).

Go here to sign up. https://bit.ly/aonsf-annual $97 per year. Less than Netflix and will do more for your relationship!

I also have other books:

The Art of Nonsexual Foreplay book 2 - A guide for women! - The partner to this book for the opposite sex.

"The Connection Code"- A book on learning to communicate better based on 5 pattern interrupt phrases and more.

Self Awareness: "BE" and "The Conversations My Parents Didn't Understand That Could Have Changed My Life" - Based on the 5 Phases to Self-Mastery Theory I developed.

And even Poetry - "Easy Poetry for Good Men" (coming June 2025)

visit https://books.by/nolancollins for details.

Courses

And a course on Self Mastery here -

https://5phasesaware.com

Follow me on instagram -

https://instagram.com/nolanonselfmastery

Follow me on youtube: nolanonselfmastery

and my website:

https://nolancollins.com

About the Author

Maybe I should have started with this so you know why I wrote this book.

My grandmother was a stickler for manners. She would stand next to a door waiting for me to open it. I was really young when she did this so I never took it the wrong way, and seeing the smile on her face and getting her polite "thank you" made me see that doing things for other people made them happy.

As a teenager dating, I often did those little things that made my girl friends smile, (and girlfriends!), and think this lanky boy with a funny accent was a nice guy.

As I got older, got married, and had kids, I realised that I forgot to do many of the things that are in the book, getting distracted with life, work, kids and the marriage.

After writing books about self-mastery, creating a book and tools on how to communicate better and a book on how to write poetry (for men!), I kept thinking about what my purpose is. I realised that it's threefold: to help people understand themselves, to help people communicate better, and to help couples stay together.

This is the first of several books on the last point.

I must admit I have a slight advantage in some areas as I learned to dance from a young age, even becoming a ballroom and swing dance instructor for a while, and I'm also a trained and qualified massage therapist! But you don't have to be either for this to work for you!

I love to see couples who are in love, especially elderly couples, and see them do things for each other selflessly.

Unfortunately I think more and more people come from homes where both parents work, and the only time parents show affection is in private, or when away from their kids. The art of connection has been lost over time and is at risk of disappearing like the dodo!

My teenage daughter frustratingly told me that the boys she was interested in had no manners, only thought about themselves or the one thing they were after. There was no finesse, no sensuality that didn't have the end goal of being intimate. For her, this was an immediate red flag.

So I've taken it on myself to teach the boys of the world how to be men by putting their partner first, and learning all the ways they can do things for their partner to keep them happier, without the expectation of sex every time they do it.

My daugher knows what a gentleman looks like because she saw me do the things in this book.

Anyway, I believe everyone deserves to be happy, and it doesn't take much effort to do the small things that help every day feel a little lighter, feel appreciated, respected and adored.

If you're a woman reading this, there's a companion book for women that can help you do things for your partner that will help him feel good about himself, the way you see him, and the relationship overall.

I wish you the best of luck in your life, love and relationships.

Nolan Collins - Author

A quick note:

This book works equally well for same-sex partners. It's all about love, connection and being there for your partner.